Hit Me—I Need the Money!

A publication of the
Center for Self-Governance

Hit Me—
I Need the Money!

*The Politics of
Auto Insurance Reform*

Marjorie M. Berte

ICS Press

San Francisco, California

This book is a publication of the Center for Self-Governance, dedicated to the study of self-governing institutions. The Center is affiliated with the Institute for Contemporary Studies, a non-partisan, nonprofit public policy research organization. The analyses, conclusions, and opinions expressed in ICS Press publications are those of the authors and not necessarily those of the Institute, or of its officers, directors, or others associated with, or funding, its work.

Inquiries, book orders, and catalog requests should be addressed to ICS Press, 243 Kearny Street, San Francisco, CA 94108. (415) 981-5353. Fax (415) 986-4878. For book orders and catalog requests call toll free in the contiguous United States: (800) 326-0263. Distributed to the trade by National Book Network, Lanham, Maryland.

Designed by Herman + Company. Indexed by Shirley Kessel.

0 9 8 7 6 5 4 3 2 1

Library of Congress Cataloging-in-Publication Data

Berte, Marjorie M.
    Hit me—I need the money : the politics of auto insurance reform / by Marjorie M. Berte.
        p.   cm.
    Includes bibliographical references (p.   ) and index.
    ISBN 1-55815-152-4 (cloth)
    1. Insurance, Automobile—United States.   I. Institute for Contemporary Studies.   II. Title.
HG9970.3.B47 1991   368.5′72′00973—dc20   CIP 91-11911

To my parents, who sacrificed for my education

Foreword

This book was written with a clear purpose: to reform the American auto insurance system. Insurance is essential to Americans' entrepreneurial, self-governing way of life, giving them the freedom to undertake everyday activities that involve risk. Currently, however, auto insurance rates are skyrocketing—even for good drivers—forcing more and more people to go without insurance and placing an increasingly unbearable burden on those of us who stay insured.

The title of this book, *Hit Me—I Need the Money!*, underscores the perverse opportunism in the auto insurance game that drives rates up. The "players" that now benefit—lawyers, doctors, and repair shops, just to name a few—all have a stake in the current system. Auto insurance is riddled with abuse: some experts estimate that a quarter of all claims contain some element of fraud. This book shows in straightforward terms where our insurance dollars now go.

How should we change the system? A few "progressive" reformers want to create a socialist-style, state-run bureaucracy to provide auto insurance to consumers. That such a proposal could be taken seriously, even by a few, in light of the dramatic failure of centralized economies worldwide points to the lack of imagination on the part of its proponents. We need reform, but a state insurance monopoly is simply not the answer.

Ideas like this stem from the great distrust Americans have for auto insurance companies. The industry has been remarkably unsuccessful in building the faith of its customers, even though it has credible local representatives, in the form of agents, who live in every community in the nation. Simply put, until insurance companies wake up and realize that they have an obligation to the community of insurance buyers to work for fundamental reform, consumers will continue to regard them as part of the problem.

Reform is a moral imperative. We cannot allow increasing numbers of drivers to go without insurance. We cannot allow the economic well-being of families to be threatened simply because small groups of special interests are able to use politics to thwart real reform. These are strong words, yet the sense of outrage this issue generates can only lead us to speak out. Increasingly we see liberals and conservatives, Democrats and Republicans, joining forces to look for real reform, based on the moral principle of self-governance. This book offers simple yet thorough guidelines to provide adequate insurance to all drivers and maintain a competitive industry that will guarantee fair rates and good service.

It is our hope that the ideas in this book will prompt citizens, insurance agents, responsible reformers, and insurance companies to demand change—now.

> Robert B. Hawkins, Jr., President
> Institute for Contemporary Studies

Contents

Acknowledgments

I am deeply grateful to Robert B. Hawkins, Jr., of the Institute for Contemporary Studies for his generous and patient support of this project. Robert W. Davis, as editor, provided thought-provoking assistance at all stages of the work. Without his help and ability, this book would never have reached completion. I owe special thanks to six individuals who provided important suggestions, information, and perspectives: Dr. Sean F. Mooney, Dr. Emmett J. Vaughan, Donald W. Segraves, Patrick J. Kelly, William B. Hussey, Jr., and Jerry W. O'Kane. Mr. O'Kane, in addition to being an insurance expert, is my husband, and provided a lot more than editorial support.

The Problem

I t is a universal experience: good drivers have seen their auto insurance premiums nearly double over the past five years. Millions of Americans now find auto insurance a serious financial burden, and they are outraged. Auto insurance simply costs too much, and many people think it is a rip-off. If rates continue to rise, even more drivers will go without insurance.

The most frustrating thing is that the auto insurance system seems beyond our control. No matter how good one's driving record, premiums continue to rise. Since 1982, premiums have grown at more than twice the rate of inflation. In some urban areas—Philadelphia, Los Angeles, Detroit, or Miami, for example—a good driver pays a premium of $2,000 a year on a three-year-old Chevrolet worth $8,000. In many cities four-digit annual premiums are common. The system does not seem to reward insurance buyers for their good driving habits or their efforts to control their own losses.

When people do not get their money's worth from other products, they simply stop purchasing them. When it comes to auto insurance, however, that option is not available to most Americans. Without insurance, many would not drive for fear of crash-related lawsuits that could render them destitute. And they must drive—for most people, driving is the only way to get to work. Moreover, insurance is mandatory in most states. Although most Americans strongly believe in insuring themselves against

1

accidents, mandatory insurance laws seem to take away citizens' choice—a value of great importance to Americans—and give the impression that insurance companies have a monopolistic right to run roughshod over the consumer. The problem with our current system is that those who pay the premiums—those who together form what we will call the community of insurance buyers—have no control over where their money goes.

As a result, people are outraged at ever-increasing rates and frustrated over the lack of solutions. Some of that anger is directed at politicians, who are blamed for failing to solve the auto insurance problem, but most of the public's emotion is directed at insurance companies. "I'm livid over what they're charging me," says one customer. "I don't think their rates are justifiable." Another driver agrees, "The consumer has no trust in what the insurance industry says. The trust just isn't there." The emotion is widespread: "Insurance companies don't give a damn about us, quite frankly. This is [about] money." Because insurance is usually mandatory, it seems like a public utility: it should be available to everyone at affordable rates. The difference is that utilities are granted a monopoly and guaranteed a profit. Insurance companies are not. What angers people most is the insurance company that raises rates again and again without any apparent concern about the impact of those huge premium bills on its customers.

The manifestations of that anger are almost everywhere. In some states public frustration has reached the ballot box. In 1988, California voters, by a narrow margin, passed a complex initiative promising them a 20 percent rate reduction. The plan did not work. In 1989, the California Supreme Court overruled key provisions of the law. Since then California's insurance reform has been mired in lawsuits and administrative hearings. In the more than two years after the voters passed the initiative, California's insurance problems have only worsened. Many voters who cast a yes vote probably saw little chance that such a simplistic solution would ever work. Most would admit that they had very little expectation of a rollback and refund. But if given a chance they probably would vote for the initiative again because they believe

that auto insurance prices are too high and that they are not getting their money's worth.

Driving is a risky business, both personally and financially. To
shield themselves from the personal and financial risks of auto
accidents, most drivers choose auto insurance. Accident statistics
show that drivers have a 1 in 8 chance of being involved in a
motor vehicle accident each year. Thirteen out of every one hundred auto insurance policyholders will experience some type of
accident or loss related to the auto during a normal year. On an
average day in the United States, 90,000 accidents occur; 15,000
people are injured; 130 die. Four thousand cars are stolen. The
daily economic loss totals over $200 million to repair and replace
cars and property, to provide medical care for the injured, and to
put people's lives back together. American drivers pay $200 mil-
lion a day in insurance to cover the losses resulting from those
accidents.

People buy insurance to be protected against these losses.
Each driver who buys insurance pays, through premiums, a piece
of the $200 million in losses that auto accidents cost each day in
the United States. How much of that total each driver pays depends on a long list of factors—driving record, vehicle type, location, types of coverage purchased, and so on. A driver's total
premium can be fairly reasonable, or it can be so high that insurance is impossible to afford. Annual premiums for drivers in
some states are still relatively affordable. Iowa drivers, for instance, have very low rates compared with other states—just a
few hundred dollars a year. But a driver in an urban area may be
paying thousands of dollars a year. Premiums in the multiple
thousands take a very large bite out of an individual's or family's
total income. For the student with an old Volkswagen worth $800,
insurance that costs $2,200 a year seems completely out of line.
Consumers want relief.

The Politics

When something in our society goes wrong, elected officials and
government employees are often expected to "fix" the problem,

to find solutions. The auto insurance problem has been no exception: politicians, legislators, and government officials have been fiddling with auto insurance for a long time. If solutions have not been found, it is not for lack of effort. All sorts of "solutions" have been tried somewhere in the country: more regulation of insurance company prices and practices, less regulation, no-fault laws, strict liability laws, state-run auto insurance programs, assigned risk markets, mandatory insurance laws, mandatory rate cuts, seatbelt use laws, and drunk driving enforcement laws.

In extreme crisis states, such as Massachusetts, New Jersey, California, and Pennsylvania, any number of ineffective laws have been passed. The California initiative promised an easy solution: just lower the rates. What the initiative's proponents overlooked was the expense side of the equation: someone has to pay for the ever-increasing cost of auto accidents. The resulting legal and regulatory mess has cost insurers millions of dollars. Eventually, this will be passed on to consumers. In another example, New Jersey established an auto insurance program with artificially low rates. Eventually, half of all drivers in New Jersey were insured by the state program. After it amassed several *billion* dollars in losses, it was dismantled. Taxpayers will foot this bill.

Why have legislatures failed to solve the auto insurance problem? The answer is that previous reforms have not addressed underlying causes and costs. Political solutions have tended toward the easy solutions, leading to aggravated crises in some areas of the country. Whenever a complex issue, especially an economic one, enters politics, it gets messy. Politicians often forget that the basic laws of economics cannot be repealed. Insurance works only if enough money is collected to pay the losses, cover expenses, and provide a fair profit for the companies taking the risk. Any "solution" that ignores basic economic realities is doomed to fail. In another chapter we will take a closer look at some of those failed political solutions. We can always learn from our mistakes—and avoid repeating them.

Politicians in many states continue to grapple with auto insurance; it is a pocketbook issue that affects 90 to 95 percent of registered voters. Insurance laws and regulations, which differ from state to state, are not federally determined; the legislature in each state must tackle insurance issues on behalf of its own citizens.

The politics surrounding auto insurance generally have been the politics of stalemate—in some cases, long-term stalemate. The situation resembles the annual crisis encountered by Congress and many state legislatures in trying to pass a budget. Many interested parties and a host of complex—often politicized—issues are involved. There are stand-offs, compromises, trade-offs, deals, and all the rest—but these generally do not lead to lower taxes, smaller deficits, or sound budget decisions.

The same legislative obstacles, applied to the insurance debate, have let consumers down. Powerful lobbies representing the "players" involved in insurance issues—insurance companies, trial lawyers, auto repair businesses, medical groups, and consumer representatives—all promote their own agendas with legislators. If an auto insurance reform proposal threatens key interests, these lobbyists work against the legislation. The result is usually "compromise" legislation that does not take dollars away from them.

Unfortunately, one of the most important "players" is repeatedly left out of the compromises: the one paying the premiums—the driver, the average citizen. Indeed, the process of political compromise is clearly less effective than we would like it to be for addressing complex economic problems—whether the government's budget or the insurance system. Seldom has a legislature passed a law that effectively lowered costs. Most often, the consumer has received no benefit from such legislation. Thus the crisis deepens.

Insurance as Freedom

The earliest forms of modern insurance were developed in London, when ships, loaded with goods for transport to other lands, sailed across the seas. Those financing the voyages sought a means of protecting themselves from the total loss of a ship and its cargo. When Lloyd's of London came into being, shippers could join together to share the cost of financing risk, the cost of potential losses at sea. Sharing the cost of financing voyages and the inherently dangerous potential for loss (in those days, losses at sea were common) allowed shippers to expand their businesses, dramatically increasing the variety of goods available.

Sharing risk is the underlying concept of insurance. A community of people facing similar risks, whether that risk is the loss of a ship at sea or an auto accident, can build a foundation for handling those risks. Sharing risk by buying a policy from an insurance company is what makes a modern way of life possible.

From its beginning at Lloyd's of London, modern insurance has enabled the development of commerce as we know it. Insurance protection is the grease of the commercial machinery of the industrialized world. The growth of the American economy into a dominant world economic power was supported through insurance. Each business was able to grow, to take on additional risk, through insurance protection. This private system of financing risk has provided society with protection that no previous social system had. The great opportunity in America to start a business of one's own, a special part of this country's history, is a feature that draws people from all over the world. This enormous economic vitality has provided American society with continuing increases in its standard of living.

What insurance provides for *individuals* within that framework is freedom. A commuter can go to and from work, free from worry about the economic consequences of being involved in an auto accident. People can move, sell a house, buy a new house, and be financially secure. A couple can plan for their children's education, knowing their savings are insured. The family whose house burns to the ground can rebuild not only the house but also their lives. The person injured in an auto accident can be compensated for medical bills, lost income, and car repairs.

Insurance, therefore, is a fundamental part of American life, a key social institution. The American ideals of self-determination, individual choice and freedom, and economic opportunity are real because individuals can conduct their lives without threat or fear of financial ruin. With it, they have

6

the ability to manage risks—to make choices about the risks they face. For the community, it allows people to be dynamic, mobile, and self-governing.

Now let us turn to auto insurance. What do people get from it? Certainly, everyone who buys it knows that it provides security—in fact, several types of security. First, auto insurance is a *liability* policy: that is, protection in the event that someone is held responsible for causing damage through the use of an automobile. If a driver fails to stop at a stop sign and is unfortunate enough to crash into another car and injure its driver, he is responsible for the accident and legally liable for the other driver's losses. The other driver will expect him to pay her medical bills and car repair costs. In this case, liability insurance provides the other driver with protection against loss.

Liability insurance protects the driver responsible for the damage, too. He does not have to pay the other driver's medical and car repair bills out of his own pocket. The other driver has her losses paid by the insurance company of the responsible party, and that party is protected from financial ruin and from the cost of defending himself in case the other driver sues him to collect damages. Auto liability insurance even provides for the cost of defense lawyers.

Damage to the car driven by the person who caused the accident is covered by *collision* insurance. *Comprehensive* coverage insures against theft, fire, vandalism, and other noncollision events. *Medical payments* are for injuries to the driver and his passengers. People buy *uninsured motorist* coverage to protect themselves in the event they are hit by someone without insurance, someone not financially able to pay damages to others. All these components add up to protection from financial disaster.

Insurance, in fact, allows people to own an automobile in the first place. The lender requires insurance to be in force on the car the moment it is bought because the lender is no more willing to bet on a person's ability to withstand the financial loss of the car than the buyer is. The lender evaluates each buyer and lends money for cars based on an assessment of the buyer's ability to repay the loan under normal circumstances. Insurance is more, then, than just security, and more than just peace of mind. It is freedom.

Insurance as Community

Insurance requires cooperative action on the part of every insurance buyer. The insurance company supplies the mechanism for a group of individuals to share their risk through the payment of a premium. An insurance company could not operate with just a few policyholders; it requires a large number of individuals who all share the premium burden necessary to pay the losses of the unfortunate few.

As a result, each driver cuts his risk of financial loss from an unmanageably large risk to a manageable amount: the premium for the auto insurance policy. The combined action of all policyholders creates an economic community in which each member is protected from financial ruin. The combined premiums provide enough money to pay the claims of the few who experience a tragic loss.

This cooperative exercise is crucial to the operation of insurance, for the insurance company does not exist without this community of insurance buyers. The larger the community, the better able the insurance company is to estimate accurately the costs of spreading the individual losses over the entire group through premium payments. The insurance company is responsible for determining each person's fair share of the total losses. Participants in the group rely on each other to pay their fair share of the total dollars necessary for the enterprise.

Every member of this community shares one common experience: paying the premium. A smaller number of members share the experience of some kind of disaster and of compensation for their financial loss out of the pool of payments from all members of the group. The individual premium payment, the cost of shared risk, is also the cost of cutting individual risk. In any given year, when the individual pays a premium and does not experience a loss, his premium dollars have been used to provide financial compensation to someone else.

This aspect of risk sharing makes sense for each of the participants because no individual member of the group is vulnerable to extreme misfortune. The group as a whole benefits from being able to manage the misfortunes of members. Moreover, each individual knows that when it is his turn to experience a loss, he will be protected.

Although the individual policyholders do not perceive this community risk-sharing element, it still exists. The risk sharing is facilitated by the insurance company, whose investors have established the initial funding required to operate the insurance business. Once the individual buys an insurance policy, he has transferred his risk of economic misfortune to the insurance company—and hence the entire community—in exchange for the premium payment. If the company's total losses are greater than premiums paid, then insurer capital is at risk, and so is the community.

The concept of community is valuable for understanding why the insurance method of sharing risk works, but in practice, as most people know, it does not function like a true community. The traditional characteristics of community do not extend to large, modern institutions and businesses. Although the community of insurance buyers does have common needs and even common experiences, and although the collective action of insurance buyers is useful to each individual and to the whole group, the interdependence and social ties of a local community are not present. Modern political and economic institutions cannot replicate the advantages of local communities: their sheer size dissolves the social trust that is the most important glue holding the local community together. If a shopper buys goods in a large suburban grocery store and receives too much change by mistake, he will probably just pocket the difference. But in a small neighborhood market where he knows the person behind the counter, that shopper would not consider keeping the extra money but would return it immediately.

The community of insurance buyers is a group with common needs and a clear economic stake in how the insurance business works and where its money goes. But individual policyholders have little control of the process. The individual insurance consumer feels more like a taxpayer than a stakeholder in a community of insurance buyers. The problem is that members of the community of insurance buyers do not exercise power or control over the decisions and directions of their community. Insurance buyers share in paying for things they would not feel a need to pay for if they could gather in a town hall meeting and discuss their future. If insurance buyers knew, for example, that only 50 percent of what they pay in total premiums goes to pay the medical bills and lost wages of injured people and property damage caused by auto accidents, they would be outraged that the system so poorly delivers what it was set up to do—mend people and repair property. And they would want the priorities changed. Presently, they have no control over where the money goes.

The members of the community must rely on the insurance companies to manage their business. How well insurance companies function as managers of the best interests of the community of insurance buyers has a direct impact on the cost of premiums. Insurance buyers have directed their anger at insurance companies in part because they do not see the companies aggressively doing something about increasing costs. What they see is a business content to simply pass along higher costs and higher rates. Consumers expect insurance companies to fight for lower rates, and that expectation is not being met.

The community of insurance buyers—those who create the pool of insurance money—is the first of two groups in the system. The second group takes money out of the pool. It is composed of hospitals, doctors and other medical practitioners, lawyers on both sides, auto repair shops, auto parts manufacturers, auto glass companies, car thieves, insurance fraud conspirators, and uninsured drivers. Each of these has a stake in the auto insurance system. Most have a legitimate role to play—the doctor who is paid for treating someone injured in a car accident, for example. Some, however, have a less-than-legitimate stake in the system— the person who sues and collects for nonexistent injuries, for example. What they all have in common is a relative lack of concern about the skyrocketing cost of auto insurance: it is not in their self-interest to keep costs down, but, indeed, to increase insurance payouts.

The community of insurance buyers has a vested interest in controlling the growth of payouts from the pool of insurance money. The definition of what constitutes fair and proper payments should be determined by the community of insurance buyers, not by others taking funds out of the pool. At present, that is not the case. In the current insurance system, doctors, hospitals, lawyers, courts, juries, auto repair shops, and a host of others determine how money is spent.

The Answers

Although specific solutions to the underlying cost problems of auto insurance are not simple (in fact, a great number of changes need to be made for meaningful savings to be found), the principles for acting on those reforms are. Effective ways to control the cost of auto insurance do exist. This book outlines the specific problems and identifies the solutions.

Change must be made at two levels. First, the individual must be able to take responsibility for handling his own risk in a way that meets his needs. He must be empowered by information to govern his decisions. Even more important, he must see the rewards of responsible behavior, like maintaining a good driving record, in the insurance system itself. Second, changes must be made systemwide to overhaul the way money flows out of the pool of insurance funds. To achieve those broad changes, the political system must be moved out of the classic compromise and stalemate mode, a transformation that will take widespread political pressure, which can come only from informed insurance buyers as constituents.

To solve the problems of high-cost auto insurance, consumers must take matters into their own hands, demanding information and a say in where their premium dollars go. If insurance buyers take collective action—especially political action—to make structural changes in the auto insurance system, then consumers will finally be able to set the priorities for where their insurance dollars go. The system should encourage even more individual control over how it compensates those involved in accidents and how it assesses fair insurance rates for those paying the bill.

The purpose of auto insurance is for buyers to share the risk of economic misfortune and to spread the cost over all the participants in the system. As it now stands, the system is out of balance but not irreparable. America faces several problems today that may be impossible to solve, but the auto insurance problem is not one of them.

Where the Money Goes

T he hardest part of my job is explaining to clients why their auto insurance rates have gone up again, even though their driving records are perfect," says Pat Kelly, a San Francisco insurance agent. "There just isn't any way to tell them why they should pay more—they feel [as if] they are being punished for being good drivers. They want to know where all their money goes."

Consumers suspect that the money they pay for auto insurance results in huge insurance company profits, and that their money is wasted because of inefficiency and excessive company overhead. They see the cost of uninsured motorist coverage rising because other drivers are not paying their fair share. They also believe that fraud within the insurance system and too many lawsuits are costing them a lot. And they have no control over all these factors that are making their premiums rise.

Where does all the money go? In this chapter, we will examine the auto insurance dollar to see what it is paying for and who is receiving the money. We cannot find ways to save money for consumers without first knowing where their money is going. (In Chapter 3, we will consider the problems that face anyone trying to lower insurance costs.) We will begin with a simple breakdown of where the auto insurance premium dollar goes, prepared by the Insurance Information Institute. The breakdown is based on data from several independent and well-respected statistical organizations that have provided insurance industry financial information and analysis for many years. Their data are regarded as credible by virtually everyone who studies the insurance business.[1]

Indeed, the breakdown of auto insurance dollars prepared by the Insurance Information Institute (III) is supported by studies produced both by consumer groups and by a key state regulator. In 1989, for example, a coalition of well-known consumer groups released a report on auto insurance reform entitled "Reducing Auto Insurance Rates: A Comprehensive Program" that included a detailed breakdown of how the total national premium for auto insurance was spent in 1988. Although the arrangement of items in the report does not correspond exactly with the III study, the consumer groups' report agrees in substance with the basic categories and amounts provided by the III analysis. Similarly, a study by the California Department of Insurance, which reviewed thousands of auto accident claims from 1989 to identify payment components, also confirms the III analysis of where the money goes. In short, each study shows nearly the same breakdown of total auto insurance dollars, regardless of whether the data come from an insurance industry organization, a state regulator, or a consumer group.[2]

For the purpose of providing simple-to-understand comparisons, we will use $100 to represent the total of all U.S. private passenger auto insurance revenue, using 1989 data, the most current year available. The $100 in revenue consists of $90 of premium and $10 of investment income, which insurance companies earn by investing premiums. Table 2.1 and Figure 2.1 show where that $100 in insurance revenue comes from and where it goes. Where then should we begin in our efforts to lower premiums? We will start with the largest portion of the premium dollar, *claims*—first, the dollars paid out for damaged property and then the dollars paid for personal injury. Our examination will then turn to the *operating expenses* of insurance companies, including agents' commissions. And finally, we will look at the bottom line—*profits*.

TABLE 2.1

Where Auto Insurance Money Goes

ITEM	AMOUNT (dollars)
Revenue	
Premium	90
Investment income	10
Total	**$100**
Expenses	
Claims and claims expenses	77
Operating expenses	19
State premium taxes, licenses, and fees; federal income taxes	3
Total	**($99)**
Profit	**$1**

NOTE: Amounts have been rounded to the nearest dollar.

SOURCE: Insurance Information Institute, "Executive Letter," May 28, 1990.

FIGURE 2.1

The Auto Insurance Premium

WHERE THE MONEY COMES FROM

Investment income

$10

$90 Premium

$100

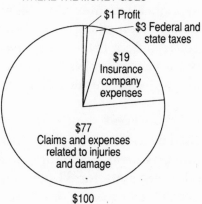

WHERE THE MONEY GOES

$1 Profit

$3 Federal and state taxes

$19 Insurance company expenses

$77 Claims and expenses related to injuries and damage

$100

SOURCE: Insurance Information Institute, 1989 Data.

TABLE 2.2

Where Claims and Claims Expense Dollars Go

EXPENSE	AMOUNT (dollars)
Payments for damage to property and cars	
Property damage liability claims	13
Collision and comprehensive claims	23
Costs of settling property claims	3
Subtotal	**$39**
Payments for injuries to people	
Medical expenses	10
Lost wages and other economic payments	4
Noneconomic damages, including pain and suffering awards	11
Lawyers' fees (both plaintiff and defense)	10
Other costs of settling injury claims	3
Subtotal	**$38**
Total claims and claims expense	**$77**

SOURCE: Insurance Information Institute.

Claims

Table 2.2 shows where the $77 spent on claims out of every $100 in insurance revenue goes. Significant savings may be found by changing something in the claims payments portion of the premium dollar, since it is the largest piece of the premium pie. The claims dollar can be broken into two parts—dollars paid out related to property damage and dollars paid out related to injured people.

Property damage

Total payments for claims arising out of damage to cars and other property break down into three categories: property damage liability accounts for 33 percent, comprehensive and collision 59 percent, and costs of settling claims 8 percent (see Figure 2.2).

Property damage liability. The first category, the individual's liability for causing damage to someone else's car or property, includes

FIGURE 2.2

Where Property Damage Dollars Go

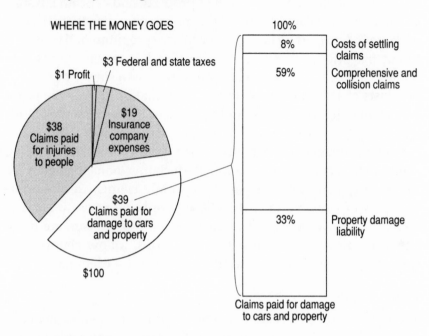

WHERE THE MONEY GOES

$1 Profit

$3 Federal and state taxes

$38 Claims paid for injuries to people

$19 Insurance company expenses

$39 Claims paid for damage to cars and property

$100

100%

8% — Costs of settling claims

59% — Comprehensive and collision claims

33% — Property damage liability

Claims paid for damage to cars and property

SOURCE: Insurance Information Institute.

all costs for repairing the other person's car, for paying related expenses such as renting a substitute automobile, and for defending against a lawsuit if the other driver sues. If something is damaged other than another car, such as a telephone pole, building, or sign, this portion of the policy pays those losses as well. It is called "liability coverage" because it protects the policyholder from financial responsibility for someone else's property or car.

Comprehensive and collision claims. The largest portion of the property claim dollar goes to direct losses for the policyholder's own vehicle, nearly 60 percent. The comprehensive claims dollars will replace broken windows if the breakage was not caused by an accident and will repair a car hit by a downed tree, damaged by flood waters, or destroyed by fire. Comprehensive coverage also pays for replacing stolen cars, while collision dollars pay to repair or replace cars damaged in accidents. These dollars for comprehensive and collision claims are paid directly by the insurance company to repair and replace damaged or lost property and cars: no lawsuits are involved, so that virtually all the money goes directly to the cost of damaged property. The only way to save premium dollars here is to cut the price of car repairs or to find less expensive ways to replace damaged cars and other property—not a simple task.

Costs of settling property claims. The final portion of the property claims dollar, accounting for 8 percent, goes to settle claims and pay other expenses, such as the cost of claims adjusters to examine damaged property and manage the process of settling claims. This cost cannot be eliminated; claims managers, who see that the right amounts are paid for the right claims, are an important part of controlling costs. These people represent insurance companies in working with policyholders whose cars are damaged, handle claims, deal with body shops, follow claims from beginning to end, and oversee the issuance of settlement checks.

Personal injury

The other part of the claims dollar is paid out when someone is injured or killed in an auto accident. This bodily injury component of the claims dollar has been rising faster than any other portion, increasing 14 percent in 1988 alone. Property damage claim costs rose an average of 7 percent per year from 1986 to 1988. During that same period, bodily injury claims costs rose an average of 13 percent per year. This increase deserves close examination.

Total payments for claims for personal injuries break down into five categories (see Figure 2.3). As a percentage of total injury claims dollars, they are 29 percent for noneconomic losses (pain and suffering), 26 percent for medical care, 26 percent for lawyers for both sides, 11 percent for wage and other economic losses, and 8 percent for the cost of settling claims.

Medical expenses. Only 26 percent of bodily injury claims costs goes to pay direct medical expenses. Translated back to the total premium dollar, payments for direct medical attention to injured people is only 10 percent of the total premium paid by policyholders. This seems astonishingly low since bodily injury liability is

FIGURE 2.3

Where Personal Injury Dollars Go

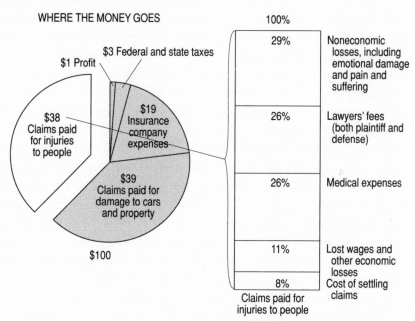

WHERE THE MONEY GOES

$3 Federal and state taxes
$1 Profit
$38 Claims paid for injuries to people
$19 Insurance company expenses
$39 Claims paid for damage to cars and property
$100

100%		
29%	Noneconomic losses, including emotional damage and pain and suffering
26%	Lawyers' fees (both plaintiff and defense)
26%	Medical expenses
11%	Lost wages and other economic losses
8%	Cost of settling claims

Claims paid for injuries to people

SOURCE: Insurance Information Institute.

the largest portion of the auto insurance premium for most people. Indeed, the main purpose of auto insurance is to compensate those injured in accidents. Given the exploding cost of health care in America in recent years, it is amazing that the cost of direct medical care consumes only 10 percent of the total premium bill.

Lost wages and other economic losses. Eleven percent of the injury claims dollar goes to reimburse people for wages and income lost while out of work because of an accident. An injured person who spends time in a hospital is unlikely to be able to work while recuperating and undergoing rehabilitation. This amount also covers other actual economic losses the injured person suffers.

Lawyers' fees. Payments to lawyers on both sides of auto accident disputes amount to 26 percent of all claims dollars paid out for injuries. According to the report of the Insurance Research Council, "Attorney Involvement in Auto Injury Claims," attorney representation in auto injury claims has increased by almost 60 percent since 1977. Almost *half* of all people injured in auto accidents talk with an attorney about their accident. Thirty-five percent of these accident victims hire an attorney to represent them and handle settlement negotiations. This percentage is up substantially from 1977, when only 21 percent of injured persons hired attorneys. Attorney representation on one side, of course, requires it on the other side. If a driver injures someone in an auto accident and the injured person hires an attorney to collect damages, the first response of the driver will be to call his insurance company and request that an attorney represent him. That is part of the coverage provided by liability insurance for bodily injury.

Lawyers actually take more out of the system than the 26 percent of injury claims dollars, however. Total payments to lawyers from injury claims represent 10 percent of total premium dollars. Attorneys are also paid approximately 3 percent of total premium in property damage liability claims. Attorneys, then, receive more of the total premium dollar, roughly 13 percent, than goes for medical care for injured persons, 10 percent.

In California, combined insurance company payments for plaintiffs' lawyers and defense lawyers totaled $17 out of every $100 in premium paid by policyholders, whereas payments for all medical costs came to only $13 out of $100 in premium, according to the California Department of Insurance study.

The increased involvement of attorneys in auto injury claims would make sense if hiring a lawyer automatically brought the claimant greater payments. That is not the case, however, since only a few claimants receive large settlements. Most claimants who hire attorneys yield a percentage of their settlement to the lawyers in payment of their fees. Insurance buyers are likely to perceive an imbalance here because compensating attorneys is hardly the purpose of auto insurance: paying medical bills and replacing damaged property is. Chapter 5 will examine this portion of the premium dollar in greater detail, identifying ways to cut some of the legal costs from the system.

Settling claims. Eight percent of the injury claims dollar goes to the costs of settling claims other than the cost of lawyers. This same percentage applies to handling property damage claims and reflects the administrative cost of managing claims. Some of the dollars expended to settle claims are actually spent to prevent or mitigate loss. Costs incurred to determine if claim amounts are excessive, invalid, or fraudulent might even save money. These expenses, while not associated with a legitimate claim payout, are included in the total cost of settling claims.

Pain and suffering. The largest slice of the injury claims pie goes for noneconomic damages, that is, general damages or "pain and suffering." These payments go beyond making the injured person financially whole again, giving compensation over and above actual economic loss. While an injured person will be reimbursed for tangible economic losses such as direct medical bills and lost wages, he may also demand compensation for the pain of the injuries and for the stress and suffering he and his family endured. These intangible losses, or emotional damages, cannot be precisely measured or quantified. Payment for noneconomic losses, pain and suffering, is usually figured as a multiple of the tangible economic losses, often two or three times the amount of economic losses.

Noneconomic loss payments account for 29 percent of all dollars paid in injury claims, not including the portion of noneconomic awards paid to the lawyer as a contingency fee. Noneconomic loss payments are larger than medical payments and larger than lawyers' fees. The III's national study calculates this category at 11 percent of the total auto insurance revenue dollar. In the California study, payments for noneconomic losses totaled 13 percent of the auto insurance dollar. Compensation for pain and suffering is clearly higher in California than in the country as a whole and contributes to that state's higher insurance rates.

Company Expenses and Profits

Excluding taxes, insurance companies spend roughly $19 out of every $100 in ways not related to paying claims (see Figure 2.4). In addition, they pay about $3 in federal income taxes and state premium taxes. Most state premium taxes are based on a percentage of gross premium, not on net income, a practice established

FIGURE 2.4

Auto Insurance Company Expenses

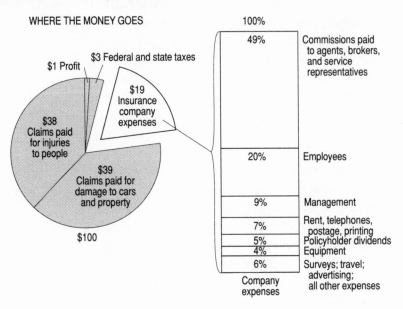

SOURCES: Insurance Information Institute; Orin Kramer, presentation to the National Conference on Auto Insurance Issues, Alexandria, Virginia, March 16, 1989.

decades ago to protect state governments from wild swings in revenue from insurance companies and provide steady and predictable tax revenue. Because federal taxes are based on the company's net income, they will vary somewhat from year to year. State and federal taxes on the insurance business, like all taxes, are unlikely to go anywhere but up and thus do not offer much hope for lower premium rates for consumers.

Where, then, can consumer dollars be saved? The consumer coalition report on reducing the cost of auto insurance issued in May 1989 by Consumer Federation of America, Consumers Union, National Insurance Consumer Organization, and Public Citizen, cites company expenses as the place for great savings. But is there really a way to reduce the $19 spent on overhead and expenses? Can inefficiency be eliminated to lower prices for auto insurance?

TABLE 2.3

Auto Insurance Company Expenses

EXPENSES	AMOUNT (dollars)
Commissions paid to agents, brokers, and service representatives	9.45
Employees	3.80
Management	1.70
Rent, telephone, postage, printing	1.25
Policyholder dividends	0.90
Equipment	0.80
Surveys	0.27
Travel	0.23
Advertising	0.23
All other	0.55
Total expenses	**$19.18**

SOURCE: Orin Kramer, presentation to the National Conference on Auto Insurance Issues, Alexandria, Virginia, March 16, 1989.

The consumer coalition report does not document significant inefficiency in insurance company operations. Although the report recommends increasing competition among companies, the auto insurance industry is one of the most competitive in America, with literally hundreds of companies competing in most states. Critics point to the broad range of prices among competitors and the wide variation in expenses among companies with different types of marketing systems. Rather than proving a lack of competition, the wide range of prices and expenses actually demonstrates tremendous competition: consumers can select from a large number of competitors who offer many price and service options. The truth is that very little in these procompetitive proposals shows promise for increasing competition or reducing expenses. Indeed, some of them, such as providing more comparison information to consumers (a good and necessary idea), would actually increase insurer expenses. Table 2.3 breaks down insurance company expenses. The largest number in this expense list is the amount paid to salespeople. Insurance is generally sold through agents, who receive a commission for their service. Nationwide, those commissions average around 10 percent of the premium. Competition and other factors over the past ten to fifteen years have depressed agents' commissions to their lowest level in history. Consumers may eliminate a portion of the commission or selling expense by buying insurance through the mail or from companies that sell over the phone directly, without agents. These companies do not eliminate all the $9.45 in sales costs out of the $100 in insurance revenue, since they still incur some expenses for their direct marketing and sales activities. Those companies that market insurance without agents, however, may be able to cut premiums by as much as 5 percent.

Many insurance consumers, however, want the assistance of an agent in determining exactly which coverages are needed to manage their individual risk properly. Although eliminating agents' commissions from the premium might save a few dollars, consumers would lose the choice of agents and agents' services. Later we will discuss the importance of agents in achieving genuine insurance reform.

Most of the remaining insurance company expenses are related to the cost of operating a business and are spent on employees, equipment, advertising, and the like. These expenses range from $0.23 for advertising to $3.80 for employee costs out of every $100 in premiums. In recent years insurers have been downsizing their operations and cutting staff through centralization, automation, and specialization. Aetna, for example, announced in 1990 that it was slashing 2,600 jobs from its national employee base, eliminating 6 percent of its work force, while Travelers Insurance shed 2,500 jobs over a three-year period in the late 1980s.

Are the insurance industry's average expenses out of line with those of other major industries? The standard measure for expense comparisons is to calculate expenses as a percentage of total revenue. The insurance industry's average expense ratio is 22 percent, based on $22 (expenses, taxes, and dividends) divided by $100 of revenue (premium plus investment income). Supermarkets operate at

FIGURE 2.5

Auto Insurance Company Expenses Compared with Other Industries (expense as a percentage of revenues)

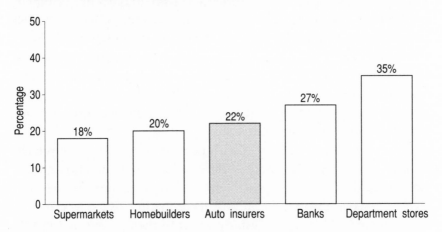

SOURCE: Orin Kramer, presentation to the National Conference on Auto Insurance Issues.

an expense ratio of 18 percent—that is, 18 percent of the total revenues of a supermarket are spent on general overhead and expenses of operating the business. For homebuilders, the number is 20 percent; banks, 27 percent; department stores, 35 percent. The insurance industry thus compares favorably with other major service industries (see Figure 2.5). Even if the portion of insurance company expense related to settling claims is added—calculated by the consumer coalition at 9 percent of total revenue—the insurance industry's operating expense ratio is 31 percent. If an insurance company could cut its staff, including management, by 20 percent— a massive layoff of workers—the savings for consumers would be only about $1 for every $100 in premium they pay. It is difficult to estimate the loss of service that would result.

Some have charged that profits in the insurance industry are excessive. In California in 1988, Ralph Nader, for example, accused insurance companies of gouging consumers and reaping huge profits. The voters, told that insurance companies could well afford to roll back rates 20 percent, approved an initiative that would force companies to do just that. The promise proved empty, though, when the real numbers were examined. The III national study showed profits in 1989 of 1 percent, while in California, the Department of Insurance study showed auto insurers *lost* 1 percent that year. It is difficult to find 20 percent savings in a 1 percent net profit or net loss. Long after the November 1988 elections, the initiative's sponsors have continued to tell California drivers that they could expect rollbacks and refunds, but they have not materialized because the money simply is not there. The California Supreme Court eventually determined that if the rollback was confiscatory—that is, if it denied companies a fair return—then it was unconstitutional.

Even the consumer coalition report on auto insurance reform identified only 4 percent profit in 1988, including dividends to policyholders and profits reinvested. Some of the consumer representatives who cosponsored that report have made a living as critics of the industry. Although they flatly assert in their report that profits are understated—without providing any evidence or analysis showing greater profits—even they do not argue that total profit is larger than 4 percent. If profits were indeed excessive, investors would be scrambling to establish new insurance companies.

As we shall see, rapid increases in claims costs, especially injury claims, have driven many auto insurance companies into unprofitability. Consumers, however, have been led to believe that trimming insurance company profits will bring them savings in the rates they pay. These promises have distracted attention from the true reasons for high auto insurance rates—the skyrocketing cost of claims. The frustration of California drivers over unfulfilled promises will be replicated in every state where rate rollbacks are ordered by law but corresponding reductions in claims costs are not found at the same time. Assuming that courts will take the same position as the California Supreme Court, consumers will get political promises but no rate relief.

Conclusion

Americans will continue to drive cars, and those cars will collide with each other, injure passengers and pedestrians, and damage property. Auto insurance will probably continue to be the mechanism used by individuals and society to compensate injured people and to pay to repair cars and property. The question is how to do that economically.

Seventy-seven cents out of every premium dollar goes to paying claims for mending people and repairing property. If that number could be lowered, then premiums could be reduced. If that amount grows, then premiums will rise. To find savings for insurance customers, we must reduce the money paid for injury and damage claims and claims-related expenses. But as experiment after experiment throughout the country has shown, this task does not lend itself to simple solutions. Not only are the dollars going out to many different parties for many different kinds of expenses, but some problems peculiar to the auto insurance system make reform complex and difficult. Some of these problems take the form of perverse incentives to drive costs higher. A thorough examination of these problems and incentives follows in Chapter 3.

THREE

The Current System: An Exposé

The fundamental problem with the auto insurance system is that there are many perverse incentives that drive up the cost of claims. Those paid through the claims process—lawyers, doctors, car repair shops, and many others—have little motivation to keep expenses down. Those paying insurance premiums, on the other hand, have expressed a strong desire for lower costs. But significant obstacles block cost control, and key parties in the insurance system have little incentive to change things.

The auto insurance system has even been compared to the government budget process, an annual nightmare that is notoriously difficult to manage. The federal budget is guaranteed to produce anything but cost savings for those holding the bill—the taxpayers. Those trying to settle on a budget—politicians, through the great game of compromise—find that it is not in their best interest to lower costs, cut programs, or eliminate government jobs. In the auto insurance system, although the individual consumer is keenly interested in lower costs, he is not in control of the payouts system. Consumers are motivated to seek lower-cost insurance but are not empowered to control the largest part of the premium dollar, the portion that goes for claims.

To examine the motivation and incentives of those involved in claims cost problems, we will look at each of the parties. In claims, we have many parties: insurance companies, doctors and the medical care system, lawyers and the legal system, insurance claimants, and auto repair facilities. After reviewing the motivation of each involved with claims, we will scrutinize several external factors that affect the cost of auto accident claims—the design of automobiles, government intervention, uninsured drivers, alcohol and drugs, urbanization, and crime and fraud.

Insurance Companies

Consumer advocates have accused insurance companies of lacking concern about high insurance prices, simply passing along increased costs to consumers in higher premiums. Consumers now expect insurance companies to do more than just divvy up the costs of insurance; they expect insurance companies to do everything in their power to control the money being paid out. In fact, insurers have for many years been openly advocating insurance reform that would reduce claims costs and allow them to pass the savings along to customers in lower rates. Why do they do this? Insurance companies are motivated to keep rates low to maintain or better their position in the marketplace. If an insurance company's costs are high, it will become uncompetitive in relation to other insurers and will lose business. This motivation, basic to any competitive enterprise, is shared by all insurance companies.

Each insurance company has direct control over its internal operating costs—out of every $100 in insurance revenue, $19 goes for insurance company expenses. A company can become more efficient by cutting these internal costs. One method, already cited, is to reduce the work force. Another is to cut the commissions paid to agents that sell policies; a third is to slash advertising budgets. Controlling internal operating expenses is essential to compete in the insurance business.

The insurance company, however, lacks direct control over the $77 spent on claims. To cite but one example, the company has no control over the medical treatment prescribed for a particular injured person; only the patient's doctor has that control.

The insurance business differs from most other business enterprises because costs cannot be determined until well after the product is sold. Even then, the company cannot exercise complete control over those costs when they do become apparent. When a car comes off the assembly line, an auto manufacturer knows how much has been spent in parts, labor, and other costs. The car maker can then establish a price that covers those costs plus a profit. The auto insurance company, in contrast, sells a policy not knowing whether the customer will have a claim and, if he does, how much money will be required to pay for the injuries or damage. The insurance company establishes a price for future insurance protection based on statistical analysis of large numbers of past accidents. The insurance company has no way to know what the ultimate costs will be for any one policy. Nor do they know for sure what an entire year of policies will produce in total claims costs, costs that result from increasing medical costs, legal fees, and car repair bills. The costs of those services are not under their control.

In spite of this limitation, insurance companies and the industry in general play a very important role in controlling claims costs. They support the National Auto Theft Bureau, Insurance Crime Prevention Institute, Insurance Committee for Arson Control, Insurance Institute for Highway Safety, and similar organizations. Most companies have also established sophisticated internal systems for controlling claims costs, investigating fraud, and auditing payments. The industry has long supported specific legislative reforms to curb abuses of the claims process. In some states, where the legislation contained real reform, these efforts have been effective. In other states, where reforms have been watered down, nothing has been effective enough to provide consumers with affordable insurance.

Working day to day, claim by claim, insurance companies have also tried to reduce costs by using claims adjusters to determine that the payout is legitimate, that the insured did in fact pay a premium for the coverage, that the policy covered that particular claim, and that the money goes for what it was intended. The adjuster, however, runs into several key disincentives to cut claims costs.

First, if the claimant is a policyholder of the insurance company (a first-party claimant) and not someone else claiming a loss against the insured and his insurance company (a third-party claimant), the adjuster is likely to treat the claimant as empathetically, compassionately, and carefully as anyone would a client. The claimant is the company's own customer. That adjuster has a clear disincentive to be "tough" in handling that claim because it is bad customer relations. Adjusters are taught to handle customers in this manner. If an adjuster suspects that the claim has been inflated or that other circumstances might cause the claim payment to be too high, he is in a poor position to do anything about it. If he does, he might be charged with mistreating a customer. To perform his role in controlling claims costs, however, the adjuster must be tough, cautious, and suspicious of *all* claimants.

Everyone who has ever had to file a claim has a story to tell about the process. While some have had miserable experiences and felt unfairly treated, actual surveys of claimants reveal that more than 80 percent of auto accident claimants believe they were treated fairly and had received a fair settlement.

The company claims adjuster has a dual role to play: he must be a customer relations agent and a cost-control agent at the same time. How an individual feels about the treatment he receives from an adjuster will reflect one of these two roles. Conflict is clearly built into the claims management systems of most insurance companies: it is difficult to be compassionate and caring in someone's time of tragedy and at the same time effectively control claims costs by being tough and cautious.

In addition, insurance companies are constantly threatened with the possibility of a lawsuit for failing to settle claims in good faith. The definition of what constitutes bad faith has been hammered out in the courts over the past ten to fifteen years by lawyers and judges trying to determine what the insurance company's reasonable duty is in handling claims. The most common bad-faith situation arises when an insurance company delays issuing payments for its own insured's medical bills following an auto accident. When a person is injured and liability for the accident is uncertain, the insured seeks to have his medical costs covered under the medical payments portion of the policy, which covers car occupants for medical treatment. If the company is slow in paying those bills, it can be sued for failing to deal in good faith with its own customer. This situation can also occur when the other car in the accident is uninsured and the policyholder tries to have his medical bills paid under the uninsured motorist section of his policy.

If a claims adjuster or lawyer handling a claim on behalf of an insurance company delays settlement for an unreasonable length of time or denies payment without justification, then a charge of bad faith becomes a real possibility. This concept goes back to the basic insurance policy, which is based on trust: the insured pays his premium, taking it on faith (guaranteed in the policy) that the insurance company will pay certain benefits in the event of an accident. If the company fails to do so, it can be liable to the policyholder for failing to keep that promise. An entire legal specialty concerns suing insurance companies for alleged bad-faith handling of claims. In response to the threat of bad-faith lawsuits, insurance adjusters are more likely to settle than fight a claim where they suspect some unwarranted request for compensation. Generally, the adjuster will determine if it is more expensive to fight a claim than to negotiate a settlement and pay it off. Very often, the insurance company has a stronger incentive to settle small and mid-sized claims hastily and close the file than to engage in a long and expensive fight. This tendency is especially strong when the threat of a bad-faith suit is added to the original claim.

For the insurance company, settling claims as quickly and efficiently as possible is good customer relations, good claims practice, and good business. It avoids the potential bad-faith lawsuit and reduces the cost of investigating and settling claims. As a result, however, many claims containing nonexistent expenses, inflated values, or small-time cheating are paid. Many questionable first-party claims are paid because it is cheaper to pay than to fund a full investigation. If the investigation were to prove nothing, then the claim would be paid in addition to the cost of investigation, and a customer would probably be lost. The claims payer has little incentive to be tough on all claims. In fact, the system encourages the insurance adjuster to settle quickly unless evidence of large-scale fraud or misrepresentation in a claim is clear.

Insurance companies are likely to handle third-party claims more strictly, by being tougher when they investigate whether it is really their responsibility to pay damages. This component is very important because investigation does help lower costs. Insurance buyers might consider what premiums would be like if insurance companies just paid every claim as presented, without ever taking a close or cautious look at what is being claimed.

The motivations and incentives for insurance companies to combat the high cost of claims are imperfect, and do not function for the greatest benefit of insurance consumers or insurance companies. Ultimately, companies have to pass on whatever claims costs they experience to their customers, or get out of the business.

Doctors and the Medical System

Doctors, hospitals, and other practitioners in the medical field have the care of the injured person as their highest priority. Ethically and professionally, they must do everything within their power to see that the injured person is given the appropriate treatment to ensure the quickest and fullest recovery possible. Indeed, the incentive is for overtreatment. When insurance is available to pay for that care, the patient has little incentive to demand that the doctor be economical in his medical attention. In fact, both the patient and the medical system are motivated to demand every possible treatment, extra tests, and the best modern medicine can offer.

Each of us, if injured in an accident, would want the best possible medical attention available. The cost is not an issue at the time of injury. Getting well, healing the wounds, and getting back to normal are the only things on the mind of the injured person, the doctors, and the hospital staff. The ideal of American health care is that every person be taken care of when sick or injured. The only motivation of all those involved in the health care system is to see the patient made whole again, to be restored to his condition before the sickness or injury.

That motivation is not naturally linked to any attempt to lower costs: the two do not go together. In fact, the drive by medical practitioners and the medical systems in this country is to deliver ever-more-perfect medical care, ever-more-sophisticated diagnoses and treatments, using the most advanced equipment. That objective does not lead toward cost control but toward higher costs for each patient, each hospital stay, each treatment, and each prescription. The price spiral in health care delivery is directly reflected in all insurance premiums, not just auto, that include compensation for medical care. Rising health care costs have a direct impact on the price increases in auto insurance, health insurance, workers' compensation, and all types of liability insurance.

Insurance companies do not exercise very much control over these costs. An insurance adjuster does not arrive at the hospital to tell the doctor that the fee for surgery and the price of an overnight stay will have to be negotiated at lower rates. That kind of cost control may occur in some health insurance arrangements but is not practiced by the doctor, surgeon, hospital, or patient following an auto accident. Some health care programs have arranged in advance the cost and use of particular treatments with specific medical facilities and physicians. But following an auto accident, the insurance company cannot specify even what ambulance company is called or what hospital the injured person is admitted to for treatment.

About the only thing an insurance company does following receipt of medical bills for an injured person is to determine if it is responsible for paying the losses and then to review the invoices carefully for any mistakes, duplications, or other problems with the billing. That simple auditing procedure goes on continually but has no impact on the increasing cost of doctors' fees, hospital costs, and other medical expenses. In cases of deliberate fraud, the insurance company has great difficulty proving whether the "overutilization" of medical services is defensive medicine or intentional building up of claims through treatments for nonexistent injuries, phony bills for treatments never provided, or some form of conspiracy to soak extra dollars out of a minor injury claim.

One other critical factor contributes to the increase in health care costs and indirectly to insurance costs. Doctors and hospitals have learned to order additional tests, obtain second and third opinions, and take other extra measures to protect themselves from medical malpractice lawsuits. On the one hand, this is good for patients because it forces the medical system to be as careful with patient diagnosis and treatment as possible. On the other hand, it causes huge increases in the cost of treating sick and injured people. All these costs are passed on through the insurance systems that pay for medical care. Doctors and hospitals have no incentive to eliminate the duplication of tests and services, but rather the opposite. For the auto insurance premium dollar, upward pressure is the result. Not all these measures should be eliminated, of course, but individuals and society have to determine the balance between endless and expensive precautions taken by doctors and hospitals and lower insurance costs. This question is even more critical in the debate over health insurance costs. Ultimately, this question concerns the next group of participants in the auto insurance system, the lawyers.

Lawyers and the Legal System

Lawyers representing injured parties (plaintiffs' lawyers) are paid a percentage of the damage compensation. The larger the settlement or award for the client, the more money the attorney makes. Claimants' lawyers therefore have little or no incentive to hold down the cost of claims. Typically, they will look at what the other party's insurance company is likely to offer to settle the claim and issue a demand for two or three times the amount as a starting point for their negotiations.

On the other side of the aisle, defense lawyers defend policyholders who are sued and their insurance company, through the process of investigation, negotiation, settlement, and, if necessary, trial in court. Their incentive is to hold down the settlement on behalf of the insured and insurer. They would, however, be out of work if there were no claims to defend.

There is more to how the legal profession affects the size of injury claims than the maximization of the lawyers' fees, however. Table 2.2 broke down the $38 spent on injury claims for every $100 in insurance revenues. Out of that, insurance companies spend $10 for medical expenses for injured people. Another $4 reimburses people for lost wages and other economic losses. Beyond that, another $11 is paid to claimants for noneconomic losses such as pain and suffering. Of the $10 paid to lawyers, $5.50 is paid to plaintiffs' lawyers and $4.50 to defense lawyers. The $5.50 for plaintiffs' lawyers comes primarily from the noneconomic loss award. In our example, the noneconomic award would have been $16.50, of which the lawyer would receive a third, leaving $11 for the plaintiff. The plaintiff also receives whatever economic awards were provided. The most pervasive practice in the auto insurance claims system is to boost the amount of economic loss so that the noneconomic loss awards, which are based on a multiple of economic loss, will be higher. (The numbers for noneconomic awards in this example are not a multiple of economic awards because not all claims result in the granting of noneconomic damages. These figures represent total dollar values for all claims; thus for any claim where noneconomic damages are awarded, they are higher than this average example shows.)

What is perverse about the auto insurance system is the extent to which lawyers push their clients into increasing the size of the economic losses. Clients are encouraged to seek additional medical and rehabilitation services, to stay out of work longer, and to do other things to increase the economic loss. A lawyer, for example, might advise a client to seek treatment from a particular chiropractor or to take additional time for recuperation and therapy. The injured person who takes that advice will be out of work longer and will run up higher medical bills. As a result, the award for noneconomic losses is even greater. The lawyer, who benefits directly from this system, has no incentive to keep costs down but a direct economic interest in pushing them up. As direct economic costs go up, noneconomic, legal, and claims-handling costs go up by three or four times. The common practice of driving up economic losses is called "build-up."

When the concept of noneconomic damages was first introduced in the courts, it was considered appropriate in cases of extreme pain, distress, loss of spouse, permanent disability or disfigurement, or similar tragic situations. Over the years, lawyers have been able to attach noneconomic damages to many less serious claims, including the "soft tissue" injuries such as neck and back sprains and various strains. The Insurance Research Council's study, "Compensation for Automobile Injuries in the United States," shows that states with high attorney involvement also have more soft tissue injuries. Clearly, the residents of these states are not more fragile. The greater frequencies of claims for nonserious injuries are directly tied to the involvement of attorneys in claims. In a system that provides incentive for both the plaintiff and the lawyer to increase the size of the economic claim to build up the actual economic losses, clients are encouraged to file claims for minor injuries.

The system enriches claimants beyond the real economic losses they incurred. The bumper sticker slogan "Hit me, I need the money" clearly indicates that no one has misunderstood the "value" and "opportunity" that can arise from an auto accident. The driver of the car with that slogan on the bumper knows that being hit by another driver can lead to a windfall payment: the claims lottery.

The single most difficult problem with the current legal process for settling auto insurance claims is the enormous opportunity for abuse, for claims to cost more than they should, and for lawyers to wrangle a living out of what should be simple claims management. The system invites abuse. Because people have learned that they can get perhaps three times the amount of their actual economic losses, each claimant, regardless of how serious the injury, expects triple the value of his loss. While the individual claimant probably feels justified in retaining a lawyer who will pursue his case and make sure he is paid for his losses, including pain and suffering, the effect is to multiply the expense of settling injury claims. All that excess is passed on to insurance buyers.

Rather than the $10 in medical expense (which includes some build-up), $4 in lost wages, and $3 for claims handling, for a total of $17, the system runs up total costs of $38 to pay the lawyers and noneconomic damage awards.

Many other characteristics of the present legal system lead to higher rather than lower costs, some of which are cleverly exploited quirks of the law and some are simply long-term systemic problems. A few are worth mentioning.

Lawyers on both sides of any auto insurance claim argument operate under a rule of law known as the collateral source rule. It prevents the defense from revealing to the jury or judge any other sources of compensation the injured party may have. A man injured in an auto accident collects his medical bills from his employer's health insurance plan, for example, and his lost wages from his disability insurance policy. These actual expenses have been prepaid before he hires an attorney to collect his damages from the other driver involved in the accident. If the case is settled in his favor, he is paid a second time for his medical bills and lost wages and in addition receives payment for emotional damages.

A person injured in an auto accident may have health and accident insurance, disability insurance, or workers' compensation insurance (if the accident occurs while he is on the job) that provide compensation for the very injuries that are the subject of the lawsuit. It has been deemed consistently "irrelevant," however, for a jury or judge to consider those other sources of payment in determining how much to award a plaintiff for his injuries. The collateral source rule prohibits the defense from introducing any information about these "collateral" sources of compensation, thus allowing the injured person to collect from other sources of compensation and again through the lawsuit award—a generous duplicate payment. Whether this practice is good or bad in other respects, duplicate payments for the same injuries drive up everyone's insurance premiums. All types of duplicate payments, whether through oversight, fraud, or application of the collateral source rule, increase costs. The collateral source rule, a particularly expensive form of duplication, is a unique tool of lawyers and a product of a legal system with a vested interest in continuing these overlapping payments.

In addition, the system does not discourage filing non-meritorious or spurious claims. Penalties for frivolous claims are virtually nonexistent. Even in cases where no settlement payment is made, no suit is pursued, and no claim is honored, the insurance company still has the economic burden of defending the insured and itself. It still must put the legal and claims-handling machinery in motion to deal with the claim or suit, adding to the expense of the system.

Finally, although some states have attempted to lower the legal costs within the auto insurance system, most offer no alternatives to lawsuits and the employment of lawyers. Procedures for quick arbitration or mediation of claims have not been effectively developed, perhaps as a result of vehement lobbying efforts of trial lawyers in opposition to alternatives like mandatory arbitration. When an individual believes that an insurance company is unfairly denying compensation or unreasonably delaying payment, no quick and inexpensive alternative to hiring a lawyer and filing a suit exists.

The legal system has one other feature that increases the costs of insurance: lawyers' advertising. No one has missed the ads that advise injured people to call a lawyer before calling their own insurance company, that brag that legal representation will bring more dollars for the claim, and that advise injured workers and accident victims to call for a free consultation to find out their rights and to get the most from their injury claim. Of course, advertising is free speech, and it is difficult to suggest that it be curtailed.

The message in the ads, however, leads to behavior that increases claims costs. One insurance company, after analyzing its files, determined that when claimants delay reporting an accident to their own insurer, costs run higher; the delay hampered the company's ability to provide quick and fair service and led to more legal expense. If claimants call the insurance company or their agent first in the event of accident or problem, the company has an opportunity to analyze and resolve the claim quickly. If the company does not give service that satisfies the claimant, he then has the option of hiring a lawyer to manage the negotiations. And if things really go wrong, the claimant can file a lawsuit.

Lawyers' advertising has heightened the perception that the average person can expect unfair treatment by his own insurance company. As we have already noted, this notion is not true: more than 80 percent of claimants believe they were treated fairly and received a fair settlement. When an insurance company is grossly unfair, it should be sued and usually is. Consumers should allow their own company an opportunity to fulfill the promise of the insurance contract to pay before seeking out a lawyer. They can also get help from their insurance agent in smoothing out the claims process.

Lawyers' ads also promote the perception that insurance claims are a lottery to be won by the injured person. They advertise themselves as the key to additional enrichment through the insurance claims system, even though their involvement does not guarantee that the claimant will actually get more money. Such advertisements promote the involvement of attorneys in insurance claims that do not merit the extra cost of the legal system. All that extra legal work leads to higher claims and legal fees, delays, and occasional "lottery" payments.

Insurance Claimants

Where is the individual claimant in this process? As a policyholder, he has paid his premium and as a claimant is entitled to the benefits of his insurance at the time of the accident. He will expect the best defense if he is sued. He will expect the best medical care if he is injured. And he will expect his car to be good as new after the repairs are complete. His motivation is to exercise his right to use his insurance. Thoughts of economizing are, understandably, furthest from his mind. He would be infuriated by the suggestion that he should carefully scrutinize what his insurance is paying for and that he should attempt to keep the cost of his claim as low as possible. There is no incentive for that kind of behavior.

For many of the reasons cited for the medical and legal communities, the insurance claimant has no incentive to cut costs related to his claim, especially if the other driver's insurance company is to pay the claim. He has no reason to help with the difficult process of lowering total claims costs. Similarly, the person whose car is damaged in an accident has no reason to find the least expensive means of repairing that car. The woman whose four-year-old Cadillac is crumpled on one side by a careless teenage driver, for example, will want the car fixed with genuine Cadillac body parts. If the windshield is chipped, the owner will want it replaced rather than repaired. If the tires are damaged, the owner may demand a particular brand to replace the damaged ones. If the car is totaled, the owner will want a brand new car, not one just like the car totaled in the accident. That is understandable.

One of the big debates in the auto repair industry concerns alternative replacement parts made by companies competing with the original manufacturers. These manufacturers have been able to make their competing parts available for 25 to 40 percent less than the original equipment manufacturer, while meeting the same safety standards. Yet the claimant may demand original parts for his repair job. If every auto is repaired with original manufacturer parts, the result is much higher costs for auto claims—a fact that may not move the claimant. The system allows payment for the more expensive parts without a persuasive justification for that choice.

Duplicate payments for the same loss run throughout the insurance system, involving more than just auto insurance policies and claims. The individual who has paid for his own disability insurance has no reason *not* to collect those benefits, even though he will collect payments for his disability a second time through a lawsuit against the other party. His disability benefits are his to collect from a stand-alone first-party insurance contract. The fact that the other driver was at fault, and will have to pay for his damages and losses, is irrelevant. Moreover, even if the insurance company is aware of the duplicate coverage, the individual will still likely collect both. While most insurance policies have "other insurance clauses" that should eliminate overlapping coverage and payments, they are routinely not enforced.

It is a common practice for a person whose car is damaged in an auto accident to find a body shop that encourages inflating the cost of the claim to cover the deductible. Some unscrupulous auto body shops also commonly have the insurance pay for damage unrelated to the accident. One of the fenders, for example, may have been already dented, but the claimant says it was damaged in the accident: the body shop provides an estimate for the whole job, which insurance covers. Insurance then is sometimes used to pay for more than the actual loss of the accident damage, picking up other expenses such as additional damage or the deductible. The ultimate costs are, of course, figured back into everyone's insurance rates.

Finally, an important trend appears to be developing in claimant behavior, especially in high-cost states. An Insurance Research Council (IRC) study, "Trends in Auto Bodily Injury Claims," was conducted to determine why auto insurance costs have been rising so much more rapidly in some areas of the country than in others. The research examined changing patterns in injury claims over an entire decade, from 1980 to 1989. In addition to outlining changes in claims frequencies—the number of claims paid per 100 insured cars per year—the report examined the changing relationship between the frequency of injury claims and the frequency of property damage claims. Two major findings of the IRC study are worth quoting directly:

> In the past decade, there has been a growing trend by the American public to file more liability claims for auto injuries. The number of bodily injury liability claims per 100 insured cars rose 15 percent between 1980 and 1989 in the 37 states that rely primarily on fault-based injury compensation systems. This increase is paradoxical, since the frequency of property damage liability claims dropped 12 percent in those states over the same time period. Property damage claims are much more numerous than injury claims, and are a better measure of trends in the underlying number of accidents available to generate insurance claims.
>
> The study also looked at the number of bodily injury liability claims per 100 property damage liability claims. This measures the likelihood of an injury claim being paid,

given the occurrence of an accident serious enough to cause some vehicle damage. The study found that the number of bodily injury claims per 100 property damage claims increased almost 30 percent over the decade, rising from 23.5 injury claims in 1980 to 30.5 claims in 1989 per 100 property damage claims, in the states with fault-based auto compensation systems.

These increases in injury claims occurred despite trends toward more seatbelt use and other safety developments that decrease the severity of injuries and indeed the accident death rate. According to the IRC report, these trends strongly suggest that rising frequency of injury claims result from changes in the behavior of claimants rather than from increases in accident frequency.

Americans obviously file more claims for injuries than they used to. Another IRC study of auto injury claims shows that the majority of these additional claims are for soft-tissue injuries, that is, neck and back sprains and strains. Most such injuries heal in a matter of days. What the IRC data show is that many more people who suffer this injury are filing claims than did ten years ago. People are not getting injured more often or more seriously than they did ten years ago, but they are filing more claims for injury. That change is behavioral, not a change in driving or accident patterns. Those additional injury claims have contributed to increased insurance costs.

Auto Repair Shops

Auto repair shops compete with each other for business, but when insurance will pay the repair bills, they have no incentive to cut the bid to the bone to get the business. Auto repair shop operators first ask whether the damage will be paid for by insurance and then discuss repair of the car: insurance is the most frequent and reliable source of payment for their services.

Many auto repair shops cooperate with individuals seeking to make claims for things that their policies don't cover—the deductible, prior damage, additional repairs, and the like. While in some cases, such as rust that reveals older damage, an adjuster can spot such deception, in most cases it is very difficult to detect. Auto repair shops are paid for work done, and the more work they do the greater their income.

A huge business, auto repair accounts for $23 out of every $100 in insurance revenue, just for comprehensive and collision claims. When property damage liability payments for car repair are added to that figure, *more than a third* of all dollars goes to repair damaged vehicles. Few incentives for cutting insurance cost are built into the auto repair business, other than those provided through general business competition among repair shops.

Automobile Design

The oil crisis of the early 1970s drove demand for the auto manufacturers to produce smaller, more fuel-efficient cars. But those smaller cars, in contrast to the tanks they replaced, expose passengers to more severe injuries and allow more people to be killed on the highways. Small cars are more heavily damaged in accidents. These factors have led to higher insurance claims payments—and higher premiums. Millions of Americans chose to buy smaller cars and will continue to do so. Desiring to operate a more fuel-efficient vehicle and cut their costs for transportation, they are at the same time choosing, probably unknowingly, higher insurance costs.

Auto manufacturers continue to respond to pressure for more crashworthy cars—cars that do not hurt occupants as severely upon impact. Automobile advertising has, in fact, begun to emphasize safety features in selling cars. The latest push is for side-impact protection, now that the debate about passive restraints and airbags has lost its heat. New Department of Transportation guidelines will require such protection, with additional safety features to follow. There will also be a push to reinstate the 5-mph impact bumper and a demand that all cars be equipped with antilock brakes and other crash-avoidance technology. All these advances in auto safety will reduce injuries, and probably save a lot of lives. Safer cars should result in lower claims costs and thus lower insurance rates. These safety features, however, will raise the cost of new automobiles. The consumer will pay more for the auto, hoping to pay less for the insurance.

The connection between safer cars and lower insurance costs is a tough one to locate. Cars have gotten smaller at the same time they have been fitted with more safety devices. The effect on insurance claims costs is difficult to measure. Leading auto insurers have tried to use their rating systems to encourage auto manufacturers to make proven safety equipment available and to encourage car buyers to choose safer cars. From a system that based insurance on the sale price of the car, insurers have shifted to a make-and-model system derived from research conducted by the Insurance Institute for Highway Safety. The effect of that shift was to recognize significant differences in the general safety of a car model in the premium rates.

A driver who purchases a car with specific safety options should expect discounts on his auto insurance premium, a reward system already built into make-and-model rating. The car buyer, however, is not currently able to compare cars based on these safety-related discounts. Consumers cannot see tangible insurance savings in return for the increased cost of specific features. Airbags, for instance, cost about $700 per new car. Antilock brakes, side-impact restraints, and damage resistant bumpers will also drive up the cost of a new car. The individual car buyer decides which of these devices makes sense to him. But society decides whether individuals get to choose or whether safety devices are simply installed in all cars. The Department of Transportation (DOT), which establishes safety standards and rules, has been embroiled in a long and contentious controversy over changes in the bumper impact standards. When DOT lowered the bumper damage standard to 2.5 mph, the uproar was loud. Auto makers said government imposition of a 5-mph-impact standard would raise the cost of cars for consumers; advocates of stronger bumpers said the manufacturers were unwilling to put consumer needs for less damageable cars first. Neither was completely right: it is a matter of balancing society's priorities.

Government Intervention

If antilock brakes could be shown to save a certain number of lives but would cost $200 to install, should a law require them? Many consumers would resent the requirement and the expenditure. How far are we willing to go to force a set of standards on everyone? The same issue arises with many other insurance-related questions. States have wrestled with mandatory seatbelt laws. As individualists, many Americans believe it is their right alone to decide whether they should wear seatbelts. The indisputable evidence of accident statistics shows that fewer people die and that injuries are less severe for seatbelt wearers. And certainly insurance payouts are lower when injuries are less severe. Mandatory seatbelt laws have been imposed in most states because people generally accept that wearing seatbelts is good for individuals and for society as a whole. In this case, insurance consumers are helped.

Laws requiring motorcyclists to wear helmets follow the same principle. Some motorcyclist groups, though, have fought vigorously against enactment of such laws, seeing them as an intrusion on their individual right to choose. The automobile driver who hits a motorcyclist not wearing a helmet, however, will experience much greater economic liability than he would have had the cyclist been wearing protective headgear, not to mention the driver's emotional trauma over causing serious injury to the cyclist. Normally, policy makers and office holders determine whose rights supersede whose. In the case of motorcycle helmets, the rights of taxpayers who pay through state and municipal health facilities and of insurance policyholders who pay through their own liability insurance are pitted against the personal freedoms of the motorcyclists. The debate between society's economic needs and the personal rights of one segment of society is far from over.

Although "Speed Kills" is the oldest slogan in the highway safety manual, nearly everyone drives over the speed limit. Speeding has been clearly linked to increased numbers of highway accidents, injuries, deaths, and property damage. The

National Highway Traffic Safety Administration can measure how many people have died on U.S. highways because they drove 65 mph instead of 55 mph. The pressure that led to the recent increase in speed limits from 55 mph to 65 mph on some highways was not created by a desire to save every life possible on U.S. roads or to save the economic costs of those additional accidents and injuries but was the result of people's preference to get somewhere sooner. DOT changed the speed limit in part to reflect what was already happening. Do people with radar detectors in their cars believe they contribute to dangerous highways? No. Do individuals believe that their own driving habits will kill others? No. But the collective driving habits of millions of people going ten miles per hour faster than the speed limit will result in more deaths, more injuries, and more wrecked cars. Government has responded to the public's desire for higher speed limits by raising those limits. Speed limits, mandatory helmets, and seatbelt requirements are all subject to the political balancing act.

The question is how much people are willing to pay in lost individual freedom, higher-priced new cars, and limited driving speed for the group as a whole to realize certain savings. The savings, however, are rarely visible to the average citizen. Many drivers will ignore their seatbelts, speed, or go without helmets at their own whim, "at their own risk." If every driver in the country goes without a seatbelt, the cost in lives, injuries, and damage is huge. And that cost will be reflected in insurance claims payments and premiums. Society as a whole has an incentive to take steps to cut those costs, but the individual may not experience the same motivation.

Highway and road construction follows the same pattern. Well-constructed roads and highways with breakaway poles, lane reflectors, and clear signs will help lower the number and severity of accidents. Fewer and less severe accidents, in turn, will cut the total cost of accidents and injuries, and will be reflected in reduced auto insurance costs. Those same safety features, though, cost tax dollars to construct. For society, the question is how to balance the two needs. If money is spent building safer roads, less will be available for other publicly funded projects. There are always trade-offs.

Vehicle theft and auto insurance fraud cost insurance consumers a lot of money. Addressing these costs takes law enforcement personnel, investigators, district attorneys, the courts, and the criminal justice system. Until recently, very few law enforcement resources and district attorneys have been dedicated to fighting insurance fraud and stemming the tide of vehicle theft. The public wants its law enforcement resources and personnel to concentrate on serious crime—robbery, murder, rape, gang violence, drug dealing, and the like. If every police officer in the country were dedicated to stopping vehicle theft, it would probably cease, and insurance rates for comprehensive coverage would be drastically reduced. But that would hardly be the best way to deploy law enforcement personnel. The trade-off is how much people are willing to pay for law enforcement efforts to stop vehicle theft to cut the auto insurance premium that covers the cost of replacing stolen autos. The cost to insure for theft is a little less than half the comprehensive premium charge. People are likely to pay that price and expect that law enforcement resources be concentrated on serious crimes, if a choice must be made between the two.

State governments perform one important function for the driving public: they license drivers to operate vehicles on the roads. Generally, the system of motor vehicle record keeping operates to keep tabs on the driving habits, good or bad, of licensees. The system is far from perfect, however. There is very little consistency from state to state in driver education requirements. Some states, because of budget problems, have eliminated regular retesting of drivers. In some states, senior citizens whose hearing or sight is no longer adequate for the safe operation of a car are still on the roads. During a recent visit to a motor vehicle department to renew a driver's license, a friend noticed the staff of the department assisting an elderly woman through the process of renewal. She clearly could not hear the instructions of the person behind the counter directing her to the license photo line, even after the directions were shouted to her. Should this woman be driving an automobile? The responsibility for that decision rests with the licensing agency of that state.

In October 1990, a ninety-one-year-old man lost control of his Cadillac, careered down a street in San Francisco, hit six cars along the way, and eventually flipped his car over. One car exploded in flames, killing two children trapped inside. Five people died as a result of this tragic accident, including the driver, apparently from a heart attack. The question raised is when drivers of this age become dangerous, what role should state governments, through their vehicle and driver-licensing department, have in keeping them off the streets? Many in their seventies, eighties, and nineties will want to continue driving as long as they can. Losing the ability to drive can severely affect an elderly person's life, causing more dependence on others. State governments responsible for licensing these drivers must respond to two conflicting social needs. On the one hand is society's need to have a mobile, independent, and self-supporting population. On the other hand is the need to ensure that only capable drivers are licensed to operate vehicles. States have the authority to determine at what age and how frequently drivers must appear for verification of their driving ability. Strict senior driver retesting rules contribute to safer conditions on the roads, with the result of cost savings on claims from fewer accidents.

The practice of "masking" traffic citations—keeping them from showing up on the drivers' record in exchange for attendance at a traffic school—allows drivers with bad records to go undetected. Most states communicate poorly with each other to identify motor vehicle records. No universal system exists for an insurance company to check a person's record in other states to confirm what type of driver is applying for insurance. Finally, no state has the means to enforce licensing, education, or other requirements on all drivers. Some people will always operate cars without knowledge of the traffic laws, without licenses, and, of course, without insurance.

Uninsured Drivers

Although it is illegal to drive without insurance in most states, mandatory financial responsibility laws and compulsory insurance laws have been entirely ineffective in forcing all drivers to carry insurance. The number of uninsured motorist insurance claims rose 20 percent between 1976 and 1986. The driver who has no license, has no assets to protect, or simply ignores the law is a growing part of our driving environment. Many of these uninsured drivers have no incentive to buy auto insurance. Large numbers of low-income people would buy insurance if they could, but they cannot afford it. The effect of mandatory insurance is regressive for low-income drivers in states that require only basic liability insurance because it forces them to buy coverage to protect others they may hit—other people who are on average wealthier than themselves. In fact, many uninsured people will continue to drive, and some of them will collect claims payments from the pool of insurance funds without ever paying for insurance themselves.

The insured driving public is increasingly infuriated by the numbers of uninsured drivers on the roads who do not share in paying for accidents and injuries. Insured drivers must buy coverage to protect themselves from the possibility of being hit by someone not carrying insurance. Moreover, insured drivers share in the losses of uninsured drivers through their liability insurance premiums. At present no mechanism is in place to stop uninsured drivers from being a drain on the insurance system.

In recent years, rates for uninsured motorist (UM) coverage have been increasing rapidly in some states, reflecting the cost of accidents with an insured and an uninsured driver. In addition, claimants are able to collect from another driver's basic liability policy plus UM coverage for losses above the basic limits. Although the UM portion of the policy premium used to be minuscule, that is no longer the case. In states with high uninsured driver populations, the UM coverage may cost as much as 25 percent of the amount paid for bodily injury liability. Without an effective means of enforcing mandatory insurance for all drivers or of removing the costs of uninsured accidents from the system, this trend will continue.

Alcohol and Drugs

We will find no complete solutions to the problem of alcohol- and drug-impaired driving. Alcohol, a legal substance, will continue to be used by millions of Americans—most in a responsible manner, but some in an irresponsible manner. Great strides have been made through several national campaigns against drunk driving over the past ten to fifteen years. Many tough laws and enforcement provisions were put in place in states all across the country through campaigns waged by Mothers Against Drunk Driving and other groups. Impaired drivers, however, continue to terrorize the roads. The National Safety Council estimates that alcohol- and drug-impaired drivers cause *half* of the 24,000 vehicle fatalities and 500,000 injuries on America's roads each year.

In 1989 one insurance company, GEICO, estimated that the percentage of premiums paid for drunken driving–inflicted damage was 25 percent, a staggering cost paid by all insurance policyholders.

Urbanization

Urbanization is a fact of life. Freeways and streets are jammed with cars. Commuters spend hours getting to and from their jobs, stressed by the traffic and long commutes and by other anxious drivers. Public transit systems are inadequate, as state and local governments struggle to balance transportation system costs with other urgent budget priorities. Traffic control systems are overtaxed, and traffic control officers overburdened. All this leads to much higher numbers of accidents and injuries in metropolitan areas. According to the Highway Loss Data Institute, as population density increases, injury and collision claims rise disproportionately to the numbers of autos. The cost of the average claim, medical payment, and collision damage in urban areas is greater than for nonurban areas. The same accident claim, with the same injuries and damage, will cost more to settle in a metropolitan area than elsewhere. And claimants in urban areas are more prone to sue, a tendency that adds to costs.

The fact of urban life is not a problem, just a fact. No "solutions" even remotely possible could be applied to the higher numbers and costs of accidents and claims in urban areas. This fact is reflected in the cost of buying auto insurance in an urban area.

Crime and Fraud

Crime, in the form of claims fraud and vehicle theft, plagues the auto insurance system. According to the National Auto Theft Bureau, a vehicle theft occurs every twenty-two seconds somewhere in this country. Vehicle theft is rising five times faster than the total crime rate. Theft can show up as a claim for a stolen vehicle where the owner contrived the theft to get rid of a car or to cash in on his insurance without actually losing the vehicle. Theft can show up as an insurance claim for nonexistent, phantom vehicles. Or it can be the activity of car theft rings that "select" vehicles to order, sending them off for a change of vehicle identification or to "chop shops" that take the cars apart, selling the pieces for more than the value of the car, or export the stolen cars out of the country. These criminal rings prosper because salvage title laws are weak, allowing vehicles and vehicle parts to be shipped across state lines with little or no chance of being traced to their original state of registration. Stolen cars and car parts go from state to state, having their titles and ID numbers "washed." State-to-state law enforcement has not yet found a reliable way to track stolen vehicles effectively—at least not effectively enough to slow the trend in auto theft. All the efforts of the National Auto Theft Bureau, law enforcement, and insurance company special investigative units have not so far been enough to stop auto theft. Whereas the trend is up for the number of recovered autos, so is the trend for total numbers of stolen cars, reflected in increased premiums for auto insurance comprehensive coverage.

Insurance fraud is more than stolen cars. In southern California, known as the auto insurance crime capital of the world, staged auto accidents, phony claims, claim conspiracies, and collusion have reached an art form. It is also big business: criminal insurance fraud rings are estimated to generate a half-billion dollars a year in claims payments from insurance companies. Staged auto accidents, accounting for a large portion of all suspicious claims, are the work of organized, professional "claim" artists, who set up auto accidents and then follow up with legal action against the victim caught in the accident trap. The most common such accident involves a "set-up" car that stops suddenly, causing the "victim" behind to rear-end the set-up car. The victim may think only one person was in the other car, but soon three or four people are filing claims for injuries from the accident. The victim's insurance company is stuck paying three or more injury claims where none should have existed. The injured parties make it difficult for the insurance company to investigate and are uncooperative, threatening suit.

For the victim of a staged accident, the insurance pays the cost of defending against the legal action and for medical care (for supposed injuries) and other expenses. Each conspirator takes his cut of the insurance proceeds. Convicted felons caught in these schemes have admitted to staging ten to twelve accidents a day. The lawyer organizing the ring will have many such individuals on the street setting up accidents.

Less obvious are fraudulent claims for phony treatment. A lawyer and a medical provider conspire to convince a person with minor injuries to cooperate in inflating a claim. The injured person may visit the doctor twice, but the insurance company, receiving and paying bills for months of visits, is stuck with bills for exaggerated treatment and extended lost wages.

Insurance fraud takes other clever forms, too. Safeco Insurance Company recently uncovered a scam in which a man bought seven auto insurance policies on the same car from seven different insurance companies. Then he crashed the car, causing $5,000 in damage, and filed seven accident claims for the same damage with each of his insurers. Safeco's discovery led to the man's arrest. In another case, a federal grand jury recently indicted eighteen people, fourteen of whom are attorneys, for conspiring to run up huge legal fees by manipulating complex lawsuits, defrauding insurance companies out of millions of dollars. The grand jury charged the defendants with mail fraud and racketeering. The scheme involved a network of lawyers who conspired to prolong lawsuits through a variety of legal maneuvers and procedures. Fraud, when paid for by insurance companies through the claims process, accounts for a substantial portion of the customers' premium dollar.

Conclusion

The auto insurance system does not deliver what it is intended to deliver—mending injured people and repairing damaged property—very efficiently. Those *paid* through the claims process have no motivation to control costs. In fact, some of those in this group have economic motivation to increase costs: claimants, doctors, hospitals, medical practitioners of all kinds, lawyers on both sides, auto repair shops, auto parts manufacturers, auto glass companies, car thieves, insurance fraud conspirators, and uninsured drivers.

In contrast is the group that creates and manages the pool of insurance premium dollars: insurance customers and companies. The community of insurance customers has a vested interest in controlling the outflow of funds to those paid through the claims process. Just as many parties in the claims process aim to take dollars out of the pool of insurance funds, so efforts on the part of insurance customers should be made to keep funds from leaving the pool unless they are legitimate and necessary.

The definition of what constitutes fair and proper payments should be determined by the insurance customers, not by the outsiders who take funds out of the pool. As argued here, the actions of many in the claims process hurt the community of insurance customers. What insurance customers need and deserve is a means for them to control that flow of their funds, a way to determine the priorities for the destination of claims dollars. That control can be achieved only through the cooperation of insurance customers and insurance companies. Significant changes can be made to the auto insurance system through their collective efforts.

FOUR

The Failure
of Political Reform

P eople expect the government to create a framework within which individuals and organizations can govern their own lives and activities. They also expect the government to solve problems. While we may have grown cynical about its abil-ity to perform some basic functions, like balancing budgets, we continue to expect it to maintain a society characterized by social justice, economic opportunity, and individual freedom. When problems arise, we expect politicians to develop solutions, make decisions, and pass laws. We want the government to influence how our society operates, but with as little interference in our individual lives as possible.

For auto insurance, the problem is that it has become unaffordable, or at least relatively expensive, for many Americans. Insurance, once an instrument of individual freedom, security, and mobility, is now viewed by many as a burden. For some it is actually a source of economic hardship. In some states the public's frustration and discontent with the price of auto insurance caused legislators, government officials, and politicians to respond. A few political solutions worked; most did not. The political solutions that will be discussed here were not targeted for low-income drivers in particular, although we would expect politicians to have worked on that problem with vigor, since the unfairness of high auto insurance rates for low-income drivers is acute. The fairness issue will play an increasing role in the political dynamics of the auto insurance crisis, especially in those states with large urban centers.

Reviewing several failed political solutions may help us learn from mistakes and messes already made. How were they created? What was promised? What was delivered? We will also look at one political solution outside the United States.

Compulsory Insurance

The "uninsured motorist problem" mentioned in Chapter 3 has always been a prime target for political solutions to the auto insurance crisis. In the early 1970s, when the subject of auto insurance first began to be a serious public policy concern, most people, consumers and policy makers alike, focused on the uninsured driver. People's attitudes toward uninsured drivers are captured very well in a letter to the editor of the *San Jose Mercury News*. Mr. Riddell writes in response to an op-ed piece by Consumers Union,

> I was recently hit by a car while crossing the street on the way to the bus stop on my daily commute. The driver was uninsured and unemployed, and was on her way home from a store. Lucky for me I own an insured car (not commuting in it lowers my insurance cost) and made a claim against my own insurance company to cover my medical bills (uninsured motorist coverage increases my insurance cost). Driving is not a necessity; it is a privilege. Auto insurance is unavoidable and must be made mandatory. Proof of insurance should be required for registration. This should be strictly enforced, and license plates should be confiscated upon violations.

Individuals involved in auto accidents who find that the other driver is uninsured feel cheated, particularly if the other driver was clearly at fault. If the other driver is unable to pay for the loss, then the insured driver, having been responsible and bought insurance, not only experiences the accident, injuries, damage, and inconvenience but also has to handle his own financial losses.

Policy makers thought that if every driver carried insurance and if every car on the road were insured, then no one would go uncompensated and everyone's premiums would be lower through the larger base of insurance premiums. Lawmakers seized on the uninsured motorist issue, believing that addressing it would help solve consumers' auto insurance problems. The uninsured motorist was a politically easy target. State after state passed laws to require motorists to buy auto insurance or to require them at least to be "financially responsible," which for virtually every driver meant buying liability insurance. By 1990 mandatory insurance or financial responsibility laws were on the books of thirty-nine states and the District of Columbia. The effectiveness of these laws is directly related to the method each state uses to force drivers to buy insurance. Enforcement efforts range from doing nothing to police seizure of license plates from vehicles on which the owner has failed to maintain insurance.

Overall, compulsory insurance laws have been a colossal failure, at least if the intent in passing the laws was to increase the percentage of autos covered by insurance or to lower insurance costs. In only a few states with mandatory auto insurance have the numbers of uninsured cars on the road declined. Studies of claims by drivers for payment under the uninsured motorist section of their own insurance policies indicate the level of uninsured driving. Countrywide, the number is approximately 13 percent uninsured. Thus, one out of every eight injury accidents involves an uninsured motorist. The percentage of uninsured drivers is lowered only by strong enforcement action by the state. Mandatory insurance laws by themselves do not increase the number of insured drivers even over a short period of time.

Compulsory insurance requirements resulted in some important side effects. First, many insurance consumers resent being required by law to buy the policy. The prudent person with assets to protect and a concern about the damage he might cause others will buy insurance. One's financial well-being and sense of responsibility toward others are adequate motivation to buy auto insurance. Americans in particular, however, believe in their right to choose and resist being forced to do something. This is a powerful political and emotional issue: choices about how to handle one's own life are added to the decisions about what risks to accept and what responsibility one should take for the well-being of others. Of course, the majority of people believe that everyone who operates a motor vehicle should carry insurance. But the imposition of a law requiring that insurance be bought causes resentment toward the insurance companies rather than the government.

People commonly believe that insurance companies support the mandatory insurance laws. In fact, they have almost uniformly opposed them. They have learned through experience the problems created when mandatory insurance laws do not live up to expectations. They have felt the negative effects of compulsory insurance laws on their relations with their own customers, when even good ones become "involuntary" buyers.

Second, mandatory insurance laws create the perception that rates are high because of the mandate. Something similar happens with utilities and other products consumers *must* buy: they see a monopoly in place of a free and competitive marketplace. Although the consumer of insurance still has the freedom to change companies or to shop around, he does not have the legal freedom *not* to buy the product. He is therefore suspicious that prices are artificially high and that the insurance industry has the powers of a monopoly—even though the insurance business is one of the most diversified, competitive industries in America.

The compulsory laws have heightened the negative public perception of insurance companies. This view affects *all* buyers of auto insurance, not just those having difficulty affording the product. Resentment at having to buy insurance and a suspicion that prices are artificially high have caused enormous and widespread damage to the trust that should exist between the individual insured and the insurer. People buy insurance for security. That sense of security is intact only if there is faith that the insurer will honor the insurance contract, that claims will be paid, and that the individual will have the protection he believes he bought. Resentment and suspicion, though, have damaged that trust.

Finally, and even more important, passage of mandatory insurance laws engendered new social problems, creating new pressure for government officials to seek political solutions. The enactment of these laws, particularly in high-cost states like California, Pennsylvania, and New Jersey, required drivers to purchase insurance whether they could afford it or not. Individuals unable to afford insurance became lawbreakers. That fact alone converted an economic problem into a social and political one. People believed that if government required them to buy insurance, then government had an obligation to make it affordable. Thus the political debate shifted from how to address the economic and cost problems of auto insurance to how to solve the social problems caused by insurance that was too expensive. This new political focus drove legislatures in several states to design artificial systems for redistributing the costs of auto insurance among consumers based on their ability to pay, rather than trying to reduce underlying insurance costs. The application of the laws of economics—not to mention common sense—prove some of these solutions wrong. We will examine this situation in more detail later in this chapter.

After decades of experimentation with compulsory insurance laws, uninsured drivers are still on the road in large numbers. The prudent driver must still buy uninsured motorist coverage on his own auto insurance policy to protect himself. If the number of uninsured motorists on the road could be cut in half and if many more drivers had insurance, fewer people would be injured—and fewer cars would be damaged—by someone without insurance. But there would be no fewer accidents and no fewer injured people. The same number of accidents, injuries, and dented cars would have to be paid for. The total cost of auto accidents, $200 million a day, would be the same. If more drivers had insurance, the total cost would be borne by more people. Ideally, then, each person would pay a little less.

Historical analysis of numbers of uninsured motorists shows that the ideal will not occur. Studies of claim files by the Insurance

Research Council reveal that uninsured motorist levels vary widely from state to state, regardless of the strictness of the compulsory insurance law, the relative affordability of insurance, the urban–rural makeup of the state, or other characteristics. Only one factor seems to contribute to higher numbers of the insured population: consistent and strict enforcement. North Carolina has the lowest uninsured motorist level of any state in the country. Its uninsured driver level is estimated at 4.6 percent, while the national average is estimated at 13 percent, according to the IRC. In addition to a mandatory insurance law, North Carolina also has a staff of 125 people whose entire time is spent tracking insurance cancellation notices forwarded to the state by insurance companies. Enforcement requires the time of law enforcement personnel as well. Those efforts pay off, judging from the low percentage of uninsured drivers in North Carolina. The question is, however, whether the effort to enforce the law costs North Carolina taxpayers more than it is worth in insurance savings.

Compulsory insurance laws, unless enforced rigorously, do not lower the number of uninsured cars on the roads. But even if the ideal scenario could be achieved, wherein virtually all drivers carried insurance, medical costs would still rise, lawsuits would still be more expensive, and prices for car repairs would still go up. Requiring and forcing every driver to carry insurance might spread the cost a little further over the short term, but it would do nothing to reduce the biggest cost factors in auto insurance—the upward trend in the cost of medical care, the costs of lawsuits, and the cost to repair cars. If savings can be found within the auto insurance premium dollar, these are the areas where real changes must occur. Compulsory insurance laws do not address these underlying issues.

Many drivers who violate compulsory insurance laws do so only because they cannot afford the insurance. The family in downtown Philadelphia living on $20,000 a year cannot be expected to spend $5,000 to buy insurance for their two cars. The choice between feeding one's family and buying insurance does not fit anyone's idea of "consumer choice." Urban areas have the highest levels of the uninsured driver population, as well as the most expensive insurance rates. The problems are intensified in cities: higher incidence of accidents, higher costs for claims settling, higher rates as a result of those two factors, and higher uninsured driver levels because of higher rates.

After years of effort in California to enforce the mandatory insurance law, the uninsured motorist problem is worse than ever: not because people are unwilling to buy insurance but because they cannot afford it. In 1990 the California Department of Motor Vehicles reported that one out of every four autos on the road in that state is being operated without insurance—a 25 percent uninsured level. In Los Angeles County, the percentage is estimated to be much higher than that, perhaps as high as 50 percent. Drivers in Los Angeles, expecting that every other car on the road is without insurance, might take as their slogan, "Don't hit me; I don't need the aggravation."

Rate Controls

California's compulsory insurance law was designed to attack the affordability problem by reducing the number of uninsured motorists. Clearly, it has failed. After many years of political stalemate, tiring of the legislature's failure to solve the problem, Californians in 1988 took matters into their own hands with the passage of Proposition 103, an insurance reform scheme. Consumers had to sort through five insurance and legal reform initiatives on that ballot, each running thousands of words. They defeated all but one, the one that promised automatic rate rollbacks—and even that received just 51 percent of the vote. As already noted, more than two years after that vote consumers have not seen the promised benefits because the California Supreme Court has determined that even insurance companies are entitled to a fair return on their money. The problem with Proposition 103 was that it was never designed to cut the underlying claims expenses that constitute $77 out of every $100 of insurance revenue: it promised to treat the symptoms without finding a cure for the disease.

Long before Proposition 103 created bureaucratic paralysis in California, Massachusetts was the scene of tinkering with the auto insurance business to "fix" the problem of high rates. Massachusetts has had the highest rates of any state in the nation for years. Drivers there have suffered these rates even though their state has the most stringent rate regulatory system in the country. The state sets rates to which all insurers must adhere.[3]

Most states follow two basic principles in regulating how insurance rates are set: the rates must be high enough to cover the losses incurred by insureds and paid by insurers, and the rates must not be excessive or unfairly discriminatory. The issue has generated heated debate about the type of regulation that best accomplishes these two objectives, balancing the needs of customers and insurers. Careful studies have been undertaken, including one by the U.S. General Accounting Office, to determine what type of regulation works best to foster competition, to hold prices down, and to ensure financial viability of the companies. Without reviewing all the studies here, most authorities have concluded that the style of regulation, within limits, does not matter. Different systems may cause more or less frequent changes in prices, or larger or smaller fluctuations in prices, or delays in rate changes, but the net prices paid by consumers are about the same regardless of the type of rate regulation.

The particular regulatory system, though, does affect the availability of insurance in the market. Any regulatory system that restrains an insurance company's ability to charge an adequate rate will ultimately drive insurers out of the marketplace. In some states a grim struggle has occurred between regulators trying to make insurance affordable and available and companies trying to make a fair profit.

The experience of Massachusetts in trying to control the price of auto insurance is instructive. Without doing anything about the cost of claims, Massachusetts began to set auto insurance rates. Insurers were not allowed to charge less or more than the rate set by the state. During the 1970s, insurers were increasingly unable to get enough premium from high-risk drivers because of political pressure on the state to make insurance "affordable." Insurance companies were unable, at the same time, to charge the rest of the policyholders to make up the difference. Predictably, losses mounted. Year after year, regulators responded to pressure to hold rates down, allowing long lag times before they approved rate increases. Many insurers pulled out of the state, unwilling to continue the drain on their financial resources. Others stuck with Massachusetts, not willing to abandon any state and hoping that eventually the situation would achieve some balance. But no such solution has occurred. Each year, a few more companies pull out of the state. Although the state has even fined insurers for pulling out, some companies have paid the multimillion dollar penalties rather than continue the economic hemorrhaging.

Now the situation has reached a crisis. The refusal of regulators in Massachusetts to establish rates that recognize the real cost of insurance has created too great a financial risk for most insurers to bear. Still, though, consumers there have the highest auto insurance rates in the country.

What can we learn from the Massachusetts experience? Regulating rates does not contain the cost of insurance. Claims costs drive the rates that consumers must pay. No system of controlling the rates charged will decrease the number or severity of accidents on the roads, change the cost of caring for injured people, or reduce the cost of repairing damaged property. The continuing experiment with rate regulation in Massachusetts should serve to point us in another direction. Rate regulation is important to ensure that consumers are not being charged too much or too little for the insurance they buy, that they are not being rated unfairly, and that individuals are paying their fair share into the insurance system. But as a means of stopping the increases in the cost of insurance, rate regulation is not the right tool. Attempts by governments to use rate controls as price controls are doomed. Not only does rate regulation not work to keep prices down, but it can have serious side effects on the availability of insurance and on the choices consumers have in the marketplace.

State Insurance Programs

No discussion of failed political solutions to the auto insurance crisis is complete without a look at New Jersey, the state with the most tangled auto insurance mess in history. Even the Soviet Union would be hard-pressed to match this economic disaster. Experts like to point to this state as the best example of how not to reform the insurance system. Nobody there is happy: not politicians, not insurance companies, and most of all not consumers. New Jersey ranks with Massachusetts as having the highest rates in the country. Although New Jersey got there by a different road from Massachusetts, the result is much the same. And the state ended up $3 billion in the red.

New Jersey used some of the same techniques as Massachusetts for trying to control rates. The state has a prior approval system of rate regulation that was used to deny and delay rate increase requests from insurers. Insurance was mandatory. High-risk drivers were required to be insured at inadequate rates, leading insurers to try not to insure them. In the effort to ensure that all drivers were able to buy insurance, New Jersey created a Joint Underwriting Authority (JUA), a pooling mechanism that required all companies writing insurance in the state to participate in servicing the drivers obtaining insurance through the program. The JUA was intended to serve those drivers who had difficulty obtaining insurance in the private market because of their driving records. Premiums were supposed to reflect this higher-risk driver in the JUA and should have been higher than in the private insurance market. The pool of drivers in the JUA would pay enough premium to make the program nearly self-sustaining. (In some cases, JUAs are structured for a small subsidy. This is the case in Florida, for example, where the JUA charges two to three times the rates found in the private marketplace. About 3 to 4 percent of Florida's drivers wind up in the JUA. The premiums, losses, and expenses of insuring these drivers are then shared by all companies writing auto insurance in the state. That is the way a JUA should work.)

Rates for drivers in the New Jersey JUA were the same as or, at times, less than the rates available in the private insurance market. Thus drivers with poor records were able to get insurance cheaper in the JUA than with private insurers. Even drivers with good records found JUA rates less than what they were paying with their own insurance company. Drivers of all types sought coverage from the JUA, not just those with poor records. Insurance companies did not oppose this flight of good drivers to the JUA because they had no profit incentive to continue to insure them. The problem that began with the JUA writing insurance for high-risk drivers at grossly inadequate rates got worse—and losses in the plan mounted quickly. Those losses were initially subsidized by drivers in the private market. But as good drivers found their rates climbing to subsidize the JUA, even more of them turned to it for insurance. Eventually, half of all drivers in New Jersey were insured in the JUA, which continued to charge too low a rate, especially for high-risk drivers.

The origin of New Jersey's problem was a compulsory insurance law that required drivers to buy a lot of insurance and included a generous no-fault provision that did not eliminate any of the costs of lawsuits. Premiums in New Jersey rose to the highest levels in the country.

By the mid-1980s, New Jersey was trying all manner of things to deal with the problem created by the JUA. The state established surcharges for motor vehicle law violations; it tried forcing insurers to cover the JUA deficits, later reversing itself and attempting to collect the money through other means. The state sent surcharge invoices directly to all policyholders in the state. As large as the surcharges were, however, they were not nearly adequate to cover the JUA's losses. At the same time, private insurers were still not granted rate increases that would allow them to break even on their auto business. By 1989 the JUA had accumulated a deficit of more than $3 billion. New Jersey then disbanded its JUA in order to prevent further deficits and to avoid the public's outrage over the state's surcharge invoices.

The huge losses in the JUA resulted not just from charging too low a premium but even more from the lack of effective controls on the payout of money from the JUA. None of those involved in the program had incentives to control costs—not the participating insurers, the claimants, the lawyers, the doctors, nor the auto repair shops. Clearly the effect of disincentives on controlling costs was acted out to its fullest and financially most disastrous conclusion in New Jersey. The JUA functioned simply as a big bucket of money that paid insurer expenses, claims for medical care, legal expenses, and claims for property damage, without any restraint. It is little wonder that the outflow of cash grew exponentially. With premiums lagging behind even a reasonable outflow of funds, the losses and ultimate deficit grew to $3 billion in less than five years.

Attacking Symptoms, Not Causes

In Chapter 3 we examined the systemic problem of disincentives to cost cutting from several angles. New Jersey put the problem on the big screen and allowed us to see a fast-forward picture of what happens when the funds entering the insurance system are controlled without the institution of mechanisms or incentives for any of the participants to control the flow of funds out of the system.

Political approaches to the auto insurance crisis must set a clear priority on solutions that control the outflow of funds, not just the inflow. The focus on rate regulation and premium controls is wasted energy. When we hear "solutions" proposed that tinker with rating systems, premiums, or other symptoms of the claims-cost problem, we should see them as a smokescreen designed to distract attention from underlying problems. The proponents of these solutions are deflecting attention away from some pet interest they have in the system as it stands, are playing a shell game, or are misunderstanding the real problems.

California's Proposition 103 is a case study in treating symptoms instead of the real diseases. It promised 20 percent rate rollbacks, good driver discounts, changes in the rating systems used by companies, regulatory prior approval for rates used by companies, increased competition from banks and others, and an elected insurance commissioner.

Insurance companies sued the day after the election, alleging that the initiative was unconstitutional and requesting that the California Supreme Court overturn it. Six months after the election, the court upheld most sections of the initiative, altering it slightly to guarantee that the rollback provision would not deny companies their constitutional right to make a fair profit. The court left it to the state insurance commissioner to sort out how to implement the proposition as amended in the ruling. Months of administrative hearings and court challenges followed every attempt by the California Department of Insurance to set rules for how the auto insurance business was to be managed. Ultimately, the cost of state bureaucracy to administer the law has been hundreds of millions of dollars. That cost, paid by insurance companies, is passed on to consumers.

California now has an elected insurance commissioner and regulations for prior approval of insurance rates by the commissioner. Banks are now allowed to sell insurance, group buying is legal, regulations for "fair rate of return" are in place, consumers are represented in the rate-making process by consumer advocates, and good driver discounts must be included in insurance company rating plans. Of all the major provisions of Proposition 103, only the rollback issue was unclear two years after the election, still in the courts to be resolved.

But California drivers have not yet seen their insurance rates go down. Why? The authors of the proposition completely ignored the underlying cost of claims in the insurance dollar. They promised consumers rate relief through simple rate manipulation. They told voters that companies had so much profit that rates could be rolled back. It was not true, and the rollback plan did not work. What really drives up insurance rates is the ever-increasing cost of medical care, legal expenses, car repairs, fraud, and theft. Nothing in Proposition 103 addressed these underlying costs.

The lesson from these three states' experiments is that political solutions that seek to manage rates rather than costs will continue to fail and should be rejected at the outset. The political dynamics of insurance reform make it very difficult for meaningful changes in laws to be enacted. The competing interests of the parties are one cause of the problem. Insurance companies, lawyers, medical practitioners, consumer advocates, and car repair businesses all have interests that do not coincide with the desires of insurance buyers. Each group pressures the politicians for its own interests. Even at its best the political process often delivers a flawed compromise. At other times we have only stalemate and inaction. Patrick Johnston, chairman of the California Assembly's Finance and Insurance Committee in 1990, commented on efforts to pass reform there, "The genuine desire for consensus legislation is more important than the imperative to reform the system." From the perspective of insurance consumers, the result of stalemate or inaction is that costs just keep going up. They are left believing that no one is watching out for their interests.

Legislatures are also constrained from making the fundamental changes in the insurance system that consumers want because the "players" in the political process control the agenda. Insurance buyers resemble taxpayers in the political environment: while each individual contributes money to a large fund that goes to pay for a lot of different programs and players, individual taxpayers have very little say in how the money is spent aside from electing their legislators. The government's process of budgeting is an annual slugfest among politicians, lobbyists, and those with a stake in where the money goes. The objective is to hammer out a budget that hurts no one, cuts no programs, and damages no politician's chances for reelection. When they discuss how to fund all those programs, the only source available is taxpayers. "Revenue enhancements" have replaced "tax increases." If the government needs more revenue, you know who pays.

In the community of insurance buyers, the same dynamics have been at work. Rather than cutting any participant out of the payout end, the system just finds a way to raise revenue—insurance rates. The increasing cost of claims was simply passed on—until insurance consumers said, "Enough!" The task now is to overcome the political dynamics that prevent tough choices from being made and to avoid solutions, whether crafted by a legislature or dictated at the ballot box, that fail to address the real reasons for high costs.

State Monopoly Insurance

Another proposal for reforming auto insurance, once again surfacing in California, is to substitute a state-administered system for the private system now in place. The proponents of Proposition 103, who have seen their efforts to control insurance rates fail so far, have decided that since lowering rates is so difficult, the private insurance system should be tossed out and replaced by a government-run system. They propose a state-run auto insurance monopoly that would be the sole provider of insurance for all drivers in the state. Private insurance companies would not be allowed to compete with the exclusive state insurance system in offering basic auto insurance, which all motorists would be required to buy.

A government-run insurance system would produce a lot of things, but not lower costs. A state-administered system would offer uniform policies and rates, and it would treat high-risk drivers only slightly differently from everyone else, insuring them at rates considered affordable at the expense of those with good driving records. What a government insurance system would *not* do is create incentives for cost cutting. It would still be faced with claims costs determined by those who are paid from the pool of insurance customer funds, not by the customers. The outflow of funds would be no more controllable than the New Jersey JUA or the federal government's budget process. At least the private insurance business, even though it lacks cost-cutting incentives within its claims system, has competition to provide some beneficial effects. A state insurance system would be touched neither by competitive pressure nor by the profit motive to operate efficiently. In addition, no individual claimant, doctor, hospital, lawyer, or auto mechanic would have the incentive to lower the cost of claims. The total cost to insurance buyers would not be lowered.

Ironically, while the rest of the world is learning that government-run systems do not operate efficiently or in the best interests of citizens who fund them, a state-administered auto insurance system is being proposed as the solution in California. Substituting a monopolistic bureaucracy for the present diversified system, even with all its flaws, makes little sense. Private insurance companies can be motivated to change in order to continue to do business. A government system would be a disastrous substitute because failure to change would not threaten it with extinction.

The very act of buying insurance is the individual's way of managing his own risk, of governing his own life and financial situation. A government-run insurance program could not possibly tailor insurance to individual needs and personal values. Individuals would not be free to operate on their own behalf. New Jersey and Massachusetts treated all drivers, regardless of how likely they were to be involved in accidents, the same from a rating perspective. Good drivers were not rewarded for their good driving. In fact, New Jersey good drivers were penalized by higher rates and surcharges unless they insured themselves in the JUA. This type of scheme is absolutely the reverse of what we want to achieve—better driving habits by everyone, fewer accidents, and lower costs. Artificial rating schemes that seek to flatten rates take away the individual's power to cut costs through careful driving. A government-run insurance system would be plagued by the systemic ills of a payout system without incentives for cost cutting and would also fail to reward the individual for good driving behavior.

In the end a government insurance system denies individuals control over their own funds and interests. Proponents of the state-administered solution argue that it would be more accountable to the public, more efficient, and in a better position to control costs. The example of the federal government's budget process, as well as many of the government programs for which our tax dollars go, should rebut the argument that government can operate more efficiently than a private system. What is needed is not a government system, but changes in the existing system that create incentives for cost cutting, both on the large scale of the entire system and on the small scale of the individual driver, policyholder, and claimant. Insurance buyers are entitled to an insurance system free from perverse incentives that drive costs up. They are entitled to a system that empowers them to control their own costs and to support systemic changes that save money for the whole group.

Before leaving the discussion of government-run insurance programs, we should consider the Insurance Corporation of British Columbia (ICBC). Some people point to this state monopoly insurance program as one that does run well. ICBC is a nonprofit, public corporation authorized as the sole provider of auto insurance in British Columbia, where the purchase of auto insurance is compulsory. ICBC was established in 1974 with the intent to control insurance costs—the same objective we have in making our insurance affordable and available. In addition, a provincial economic motivation was involved: to end the large flow of money from British Columbia to insurance companies in Toronto and the United States.

During its early years, the ICBC "Auto Plan" charged rates that lagged behind losses, causing a significant deficit. The first ten years of operation were tumultuous, particularly as different political parties came and went from power. Eventually, however, the Auto Plan established itself on a solid financial footing, mostly by dramatically increasing rates, and began to operate as a business.

The compulsory insurance law in British Columbia is more than a legal requirement to buy insurance, since registration of a vehicle is handled in the same transaction as purchasing insurance. An Auto Plan agent handles the dual transaction. License plates, a certificate of vehicle registration, and the insurance certificate are issued simultaneously. The only uninsured vehicles in the province are either from outside British Columbia, or they are unregistered and unlicensed, and are therefore very easy to spot.

The ICBC rewards drivers with good records with discounts and penalizes poor driving records with surcharges. The ICBC has an excellent working relationship with the motor vehicle department, sharing computer information on drivers. All claims are required to be reported directly to the ICBC's claims service and are handled quickly. Few claims ever involve legal action. The ICBC invests millions of dollars each year in safety and education programs, promoting use of seatbelts, training youthful drivers, and attacking drunk driving.

The Auto Plan works because after years of effort the program has developed a businesslike operation. It features rates that vary by driver behavior, a consumer education program, and tight control of claims payments. It can neither operate at a loss nor charge inadequate rates. While it is not much cheaper than private insurance, and participants have made significant trade-offs for its operation, it is a system that works, and consumers and insurance brokers, who act as agents in handling various ICBC transactions, are content to leave it in place.

Would a system like that work in the United States? The British Columbia system works because citizens there have been willing to make certain trade-offs. Would citizens in the United States be willing to do the same? Let us examine that question.

First, very few claims in British Columbia involve attorneys. In America, we exercise our right to hire a lawyer far more frequently, resulting in much higher auto claims costs. Second, although brokers handle the transactions for clients, they are not involved in insurance renewals or in the claims process. While this procedure is less expensive, it denies consumers the service typically provided by an insurance agent in the United States. Moreover, anyone filing a claim who is determined to have been using alcohol or drugs can have his claim entirely denied by the ICBC adjuster.

Our costs here in the United States are much higher, too, because of our greater population and urban density. Safety and education programs cost approximately $4 million per year for ICBC; a corresponding program in California would cost more than $30 million. Canada's government-run health insurance system works hand in hand with ICBC to coordinate medical benefits and eliminate duplicate payments. Many types of treatment commonly provided in the United States are simply not allowed under the ICBC Auto Plan or are unavailable in Canada.

ICBC works adequately, given its structure, to control administrative and legal costs and to coordinate payment of medical benefits. If those same elements were in place in any state south of the Canadian border, insurance consumers would see similar efficiencies. *It is not the government monopoly aspect of the system that makes it work, however, but the restraints on costs built into the system.* On an apples-to-apples basis, ICBC auto insurance rates are not lower than rates for similar demographic areas of the United States.

The 1989 Annual Report of the ICBC states that its premiums continue to rise because of increased claims costs—auto repair bills, rehabilitation costs, medical expenses, and legal settlements are all escalating. The report cites alcohol-related accidents as a top contributor to cost problems. All that sounds familiar. The danger in trying to recreate the ICBC Auto Plan in the United States is that the system would be set up without the capacity to eliminate some of the very things that, as we have seen, make auto insurance expensive in the United States—high levels of attorney involvement in the claims process, widespread duplication of payments for benefits, and pain-and-suffering awards on top of economic loss payments. In short, any political solution to high auto insurance costs that proposes to substitute a state-administered program for the present system will not be able to deliver cost savings to consumers unless drastic changes occur in the way payments are made—and that requires decisions about what consumers will have to give up.

Even with these reforms, Americans would not likely prefer the British Columbia system. In the United States there is a tradition of individual liberty that runs counter to many of the Canadian policies. Are Americans willing to give up the service and advice of their insurance agent? Are they willing to accept a bare-bones health care system and limits on treatments payable under their policies? Most important, are they willing to give up the range of choices offered by our private, competitive insurance system? The key to American auto insurance reform is lowering the underlying cost of the current system while keeping its wide variety of consumer options.

Conclusion

The key reason that legislatures have failed to resolve the auto insurance problem is that any legislator who advocates a proposal that cuts somebody out of the payment end of the system is accused of taking away someone's rights and of insensitivity to injured victims. The legislator advocating the rights of insurance buyers is painted as one who hurts consumers and does not care about their needs, despite his attempts to help the larger community of insurance buyers reduce costs.

That dynamic of the political system will change when office holders get more pressure from the community of insurance buyers than they do from those whose payouts from claims dollars would be reduced. To get to that point, insurance buyers must be informed about what they can do and why it is in their interests to do it. Customers must have a clear understanding of how the claims payout side of the system can be changed. That is the subject for Chapters 5 and 6.

The Accident Industry

Is there a connection between the current U.S. lawsuit system—which has been called a lottery by some people—and increasing insurance rates? The debate about the "lawsuit crisis" has been going on for years, with controversy over whether such a crisis exists at all and if so, how much it costs consumers, taxpayers, and businesses. The civil justice system exists for several reasons: to establish responsibility, to provide compensation for the damage caused by others, to punish wrongdoers, and to deter future harmful activities. Does it do these things effectively?

Everyone has the right to sue and to go to court. And every person is threatened by the possibility of being sued and being taken to court as a defendant in a civil suit. Individuals, doctors, school districts, clubs, churches, day care centers, hospitals, restaurants, cities, and counties—every person, every business, every organization faces the threat of suit. The civil justice system, established to allow citizens a redress without resort to the criminal justice system, is our way of handling arguments among individuals that can't be resolved in other ways.

Americans are exercising their right to sue with greater and greater frequency. And increasingly they rely on liability insurance to protect against the threat of suit and responsibility for causing harm to someone else. This insurance pays for two things—the amount of any settlements, awards, and judgments and the cost to defend the person or organization sued. Liability insurance premiums reflect the cost of those two things.[4]

Why, then, the big debate about civil justice reform and liability insurance costs? Very simply, rates have soared for many kinds of liability insurance. The premium payers are distressed at the unpredictability of all kinds of liability insurance premiums, not just for auto insurance. Moreover, it is not the premiums alone that are unpredictable but also the outcome of lawsuits.

None of us can foresee when we may cause an accident or what type of accident or injury we may cause. We cannot foresee the results of even a minor rear-end collision, which can range from simple car repairs to a major lawsuit alleging permanent neck and back injuries. While we buy liability insurance to protect us against that uncertainty, even with insurance, we cannot know if we have purchased enough. We could be sued and find that the award exceeds our policy limits. When insurance agents are asked how much liability insurance a person should buy, the response could just as well be that a person can never have too much liability insurance because liability is unpredictable.

The injured person who sues faces uncertainties as well. In a typical case, a woman filed suit for injuries received in a car accident, alleging the other party at fault. The insurance company defending the suit offered to settle before going to trial for $235,000. The woman refused the settlement, however, and the case went to jury trial. The jury decided the accused person was not liable and awarded nothing. The tragedy for the injured woman was that she was left with the balance of her unpaid medical bills, which were more than covered by the settlement offer, and her legal expenses. Her lawyer did not receive a contingency fee, but as plaintiff, she was still responsible for other expenses related to bringing the lawsuit. In addition, she suffered the stress of worrying about the suit, wondering what its outcome would be.

A lawsuit carries no guarantee. Sometimes, the lawyers collect more from a claim than the injured person they are representing. One insurance company claims manager told of a typical minor injury case in which the legal expenses consumed so much of the award that not enough money was left to pay the medical bills of the injured man. In this case, where both drivers were partially at fault, the injured person claimed $3,000 in medical and other economic damages against the company, and the lawyer requested a total settlement package of $10,000. Since both drivers were partly at fault, the award was for half the $10,000 in damages, so the company paid $5,000 to the injured party. The lawyer's contingency fee of 40 percent consumed $2,000, and other legal expenses, which the plaintiff is responsible for under most contingency fee contracts, consumed another $1,500. That left only $1,500 for the injured person, who had already run up medical and other bills of $3,000. After all the delay, uncertainty, and haggling of the lawsuit, the injured person came out on the short end.

The lawsuit system has been referred to as a lottery, because some individuals have been awarded big settlements. Like all lotteries, however, many people lose. The unpredictability of lawsuits forces people to protect themselves with liability insurance—and the cost of that has been rising steadily. A closer look at lawsuits shows that cost increases are due not only to the greater numbers of lawsuits being filed but also to the larger size of settlements and verdicts.

The Rand Corporation's Institute for Civil Justice tracked $1 million verdicts in the Chicago area from 1960 to 1984. The study found that the number of such verdicts increased from two per year to sixty, an increase of well over 3,000 percent. The Rand study also examined the percentage of all money paid out in $1 million-plus verdicts. Large verdicts of more than $1 million represented 85 percent of all the money paid as a result of lawsuits by the early 1980s, up from only 4 percent in the early 1960s. The study results were adjusted for inflation.

Jury Verdict Research, a company that tracks trends in personal injury litigation, reported that in 1980, 134 lawsuits in the United States resulted in plaintiff awards of more than $1 million. By 1985, that number had grown to 488—an increase of 264 percent.

Research compiled by the Insurance Research Council, based on data from 200,000 households polled by National Family Opinion, Inc., shows that the average economic loss (medical expense, lost wages, and other expenses not including car repairs) was $4,355 per individual in 1986. In 1977, that average was only $1,179 per person, representing an increase of 269 percent. This increase is far greater than the rise in medical care costs (114 percent) or in the consumer price index (78 percent) for that same nine-year period. Significantly, the IRC study demonstrates that the dramatic escalation in costs attributed to auto accident injuries that show up in injury claims is well beyond the actual increases in medical care or consumer prices.

The Rand Corporation's study of Chicago lawsuits showed that the average award in a lawsuit in the early 1960s was $57,000, increasing to over $250,000 by the early 1980s. These increases cannot be explained away as a result of inflation because the figures have been adjusted to account for it. Thus, in two decades the average amount of a lawsuit award increased by 340 percent.

The total dollars paid out in lawsuits has increased dramatically. Many governmental entities are self-insured, and their payments for liability claims demonstrate the trend. From 1980 to 1985, when population growth was 5 percent, the total dollar value of claims payments in New York City increased by 65 percent; for California, the increase during that same period was 120 percent.

In addition, the number of lawsuits filed has also been growing. For auto accident liability, the number of suits filed has grown tremendously, while increases in the number of accidents have matched the growth of the population and numbers of vehicles on the road. In California, for example, before 1980 lawsuit filings in auto accident cases roughly followed population growth. Since 1981 these lawsuit filings have increased by more than 50 percent. In Los Angeles County alone, for example, during fiscal year 1987–88 the number of lawsuits filed grew by 60 percent.

The costs of the lawsuit system are not generated only by cases that proceed all the way through to a trial and verdict. In fact, in most cases, suits are settled long before the final step of a trial by jury. How important are lawsuits to accounting for the astronomical cost increases in liability insurance? The attorney involvement in settling the financial aspects of an accident dispute is the key factor driving these increases.

Involvement of Lawyers

The involvement of lawyers and the legal apparatus in settling auto claims has now become routine. Previously, lawyers participated in only the most complicated, serious, and important accident cases. Today they are increasingly brought in for routine cases with relatively minor damage and simple questions of responsibility. Some argue that those who are injured or suffer damage need a lawyer to be treated well by the other person's insurance company. Lawyers' advertising also continually repeats the theme that to get the most from an injury claim, a person needs a lawyer. Whatever the reasons, more people today are being represented by attorneys in auto accident claims than ever before.

The IRC study provides several important pieces of information. First, attorney involvement in auto injury claims increased almost 60 percent from 1977 to 1986. In the auto insurance "crisis" states, this increase is even more dramatic. In 1986, attorneys were involved in 35 percent of all injury cases nationwide. In New Jersey, however, the percentage was 57 percent in 1986. For all cases nationwide, where the economic losses were over $1,000, attorneys were involved in 57 percent of auto injury cases. When economic losses exceeded $5,000, attorneys were involved in 70 percent of cases. Urban households were also more likely to hire an attorney (39 percent overall) than households in small towns or rural areas (27 percent). By 1987, attorneys were hired by almost 45 percent of all individuals who received payments for injuries related to an auto accident.

How does the involvement of attorneys affect how much compensation accident victims received from their own case? And how satisfied are those individuals with the services of their lawyer? The National Family Opinion/IRC data reveal some interesting things about attorney representation. Seventy-five percent of those who hired an attorney were satisfied with the performance of their attorney. Fifty-eight percent of those represented by an attorney were satisfied with the settlement they received. But 80 percent of those who did *not* hire an attorney were satisfied with the settlement they received.

Households that hired attorneys had a much longer wait for final resolution of their claim; indeed, 44 percent of claims where the injured person was represented by an attorney were still not settled after a full year. Only 5.5 percent of those claimants who did *not* hire an attorney were still waiting for resolution of the claim after one year.

One final comparison of cases with and without attorney involvement comes from an IRC study of accidents in which the injured person suffered a fracture of a weight-bearing bone (Figure 5.1). Gross settlement with an attorney representing the injured person in negotiations was $26,728. Of that, $8,286 was spent on the attorney's fee and other legal expenses, $13,275 was spent on medical expenses and other economic losses, and a net payment beyond that of $5,167 was made to the claimant. In similar cases where settlement negotiations did not involve an attorney, the gross settlement was $16,075. Out of that, $8,464 was spent on medical and other economic losses, and $7,611 was paid to the claimant.

This comparison reveals three things. First, claims involving attorneys were settled for gross claims dollars that were 66 percent higher than similar claims where no lawyers were involved, but most of the difference was consumed by the legal expense and lawyers' fees. Second, the actual amount spent for medical treatment and other economic losses was higher with attorney involvement, even though similar types of injuries were treated to the claimant's satisfaction with or without attorney involvement. Third, the injured person received more money from the settlement when *not* represented by an attorney.

Clearly, when lawyers are involved in auto accident claims, total costs are higher. On average, though, claimants receive *lower* net payments. Further, there is a relationship between higher overall economic payments and attorney involvement, the "build-up" phenomenon discussed in Chapter 3.

FIGURE 5.1

Average Settlements for Fracture of Weight-Bearing Bone (with and without attorneys)

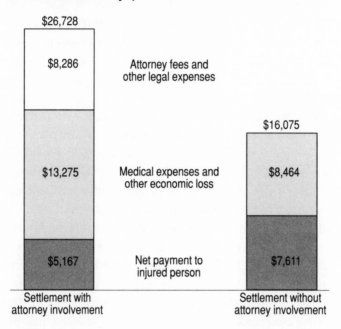

SOURCE: *Compensation for Automobile Injuries in the United States* (Oak Brook, Ill.: All-Industry Research Advisory Council, 1989).

These facts raise questions about the value consumers receive from attorney involvement. Why do people injured in auto accidents hire lawyers as often as they do? Would individuals continue to hire attorneys so frequently if they knew that, on average, they are likely to get less from their accident settlement and that it would take longer to receive that settlement? Let us review the underlying reasons people rely on the civil justice system for resolving auto accident disputes.

The Civil Justice System

The four basic purposes of the civil justice system are to determine who is responsible for a wrong, to provide economic compensation to those injured, to punish wrongdoers, and to deter future similar wrongful action. How effective is the traditional liability system in accomplishing these objectives for auto accident victims?

Unquestionably, when someone is clearly at fault for an accident and not willing to accept responsibility for causing an accident and injuring other people, those injured have no choice but to sue to obtain a ruling that the other person is responsible and must pay. There the participation of the lawyer is essential. Or when an insurance company delays payment for or refuses to pay an apparently legitimate claim for damages, chasing down that payment for the injured person is a job for an attorney. The legal system can also play an important role in complex situations involving many cars, a difficult determination of what really caused the accident, or cases of conflicting claims. Usually, however, the task of deciding who was principally at fault and who will be responsible is not difficult. In most cases of clear liability, determining responsibility for payment through the legal system is costly and slow. Even when both drivers contributed to the crash, they can spend a lot of money and time wrangling over who was 40 percent and who was 60 percent at fault before anyone gets paid for his losses. While the present legal system handles this first objective adequately, the cost is high and justice is slow. Designating responsibility and deciding who pays how much could be handled more cost efficiently, effectively, and quickly without involving lawyers and the legal system.

The second objective of the system, to provide economic compensation to those who are injured, is usually accomplished through liability insurance, with or without attorneys. In some instances, attorneys will get more for their clients than the client would have received without the assistance of his lawyer. In many other cases, however, the injured victim will receive more without the attorney. The payment for actual economic damages comes about in a satisfactory way to claimants regardless of the presence of attorneys, unless someone refuses to accept responsibility. Most claims for bodily injury are settled for under $5,000. In many cases the only economic loss is a checkup with a physician or a few days off work. Bringing attorneys into so many of these minor injury claims simply drives up the cost of settling.

Attorney representation does little for the average claimant with a minor injury.

The third objective of the civil justice system, to punish wrongdoers, is an interesting issue. Those individuals ruled at fault in an auto accident are the wrongdoers. Except in unusual cases, auto crashes are not the result of intentional wrong committed by the person at fault, but are simply accidents. No one, except a criminal involved in deliberately staging auto accidents for profit, wants to get into a car crash. The notion of the at-fault driver as a culpable wrongdoer attaches stiff moral judgment to what is usually an unintentional act. Except when a driver knowingly and negligently puts others at risk, such as when he drives intoxicated, the fault-based liability system inappropriately judges people guilty of a wrongful and hurtful act when the damage was in fact the result of pure accident. The civil justice system seeks to "punish" this accidental wrongdoer for the harm he has caused someone else.

With millions of cars on the road, some of them are certain to collide, as they do every day. The concept of punishment makes the most sense in cases involving drunk driving, reckless driving, knowingly driving unsafe equipment, or other behavior with clearly foreseeable potential to endanger other people and property.

The remedy dealt out by the civil justice system in most auto accident cases is the award of monetary damages to cover economic loss and noneconomic claims for pain and suffering. The award can also be for a third type of compensation: punitive damages over and above the other two types of awards as an extra measure of punishment. Although punitive damages should be reserved for the most serious and willful wrongs, lawyers will often sue for them in cases where serious and intentional wrongful acts were not committed. For some lawyers, punitive damages are just another source of payment for them.

How effective are the settlements, awards, and verdicts in punishing "wrongdoers"? For those who buy liability insurance, the cost of a settlement or verdict is paid by the insurance company. Where is the punishment value? The person responsible for causing the accident is not really forced to pay for the damage he caused, at least not through the settlement of claims. Although such a person may see his insurance rates go up and, if he has a pattern of causing accidents, may find it difficult to obtain insurance, this can be accomplished without anyone going to court or hiring a lawyer. As an instrument of punishment, the civil justice system is neither an effective nor an appropriate means of dealing with driving behavior, other than in the obvious cases of gross negligence, drunk driving, or recklessness. For those serious wrongs, as long as insurance pays the injured party, the real wrongdoer escapes punishment.

The fourth objective of the civil justice system is to deter similar "wrongful" acts. If most auto accidents are truly accidental in nature, then very few can be deterred. While perhaps the at-fault driver may drive more carefully, his caution is more likely the result of his trauma over causing the accident and hurting someone else than the result of the claims process, the lawsuit, or the settlement. Because most drivers do not want to be involved in accidents in the first place, the notion that a claims settlement will deter drivers from getting into accidents is silly: they are already motivated to avoid them. A really bad driver might be deterred from causing accidents by having his license revoked or his car impounded, but not by a claim against him. The civil justice system in auto accidents is not a useful deterrent to the wrongful acts that cause car accidents, injuries, and property damage.

If the civil justice system in auto accident cases is not performing its essential mission efficiently on behalf of claimants and defendants, why hasn't it been reformed? Very simply, the system serves the interests of those who benefit from the lawsuits. Personal injury attorneys have built an entire business—the accident industry—on claims, and auto accident cases are the bread and butter for most practicing personal injury trial lawyers.

The immense growth in lawsuits stemming from auto accidents and other types of personal injuries can be traced directly to increases in the number of lawyers. The ranks of lawyers looking for cases to handle have swelled in the past twenty years; the number of practicing attorneys doubled from 1970 to 1985. In lawsuit-

ridden California, for example, membership in the state bar increased from 15,000 in 1950 to 50,000 in 1975 to 118,000 in 1989.

All types of liability insurance premiums reflect directly the
cost of all this litigation. Taxpayers also feel the direct costs of the
legal system, since they pay for courts, judges, trials, bailiffs,
court reporters, clerks, offices, and for awards against government entities that are "self-insured." It is estimated that the cost
for staff and overhead for one courtroom per year in a metropolitan area is $400,000. Most urban counties have fifty to one hun-
dred courtrooms in operation. Nationwide, the civil lawsuit
system produces immense costs to taxpayers and society.

In the premium dollar for auto insurance, direct legal expense
represents more than 10 percent. Indirectly, the legal system is
responsible for slower claims settlement, built-up economic
losses, and large noneconomic loss settlements. It is an inefficient
and costly method of determining responsibility and damages.
We all pay for this legal overhead brought on by the auto accident
claims system.

Insurance buyers would obviously benefit if this legal overhead were eliminated or at least substantially trimmed. This ave-
nue to less expensive auto insurance has not been taken because
of political roadblocks in the way. Legislative battles have been
fought in many states over proposed reforms designed to correct
this runaway legal overhead. Proposals have taken many forms:
limits on awards, prohibitions on certain types of awards, myriad
procedural changes, caps on lawyers' fees, time limits on certain
parts of the legal process, changes in trial procedures, elimination
of certain types of suits from the civil lawsuit system, and so on.

The trial lawyer lobby in every state, however, is among the
most potent political forces to be reckoned with. Lawyers, who
make a living as persuaders in court, have proved to be equally
effective at political persuasion. Because of their power, they are
usually able to kill most efforts at reform early on. In California in
1990, they were even able to kill a bill sponsored by Consumers
Union designed to provide low-cost, no-frills auto insurance for
low-income drivers who cannot afford insurance. If they cannot
kill an "undesirable" bill outright, they gut any real reform as a

new bill is being drafted in legislative committee or as it moves through the legislative process. In the event that some law is passed that would limit lawyers' practice in civil lawsuits, lawyers go to work in the courts, quickly challenging the new law on constitutional grounds and chipping away at it through individual case decisions. They are usually successful. As a result, many efforts at legislative reform have actually increased the complexity and length of legal maneuvers, raising rather than lowering costs. The shifting rules of the trial process, which change from jurisdiction to jurisdiction, from judge to judge, and from jury to jury, allow lawyers to continue their work without risk of real change in the system.

Finally, the legal fraternity always has one very emotional argument to employ, an argument that has proved very effective in stopping significant reforms. Personal injury attorneys represent injured people in a struggle to obtain compensation for those unfortunate individuals. Proposals for legal reform are always met with the argument that the specific proposal will take away the rights of injured victims, either by denying them competent legal representation or by limiting their opportunity for compensation. Taking away people's rights is something we simply do not do in this country. This argument has proved very effective in ending the debate on many reforms.

The economic self-interest of lawyers in the present system has made them very effective protectors of that system, with political power unmatched in the reform war. When they lose a political battle, they undermine the reform through court challenges and case law, attempting to take the high ground in the debate about individual rights and care of injured people. Successfully self-cast as the protectors of victims' rights, they wage a political battle to protect their own interests. As a result, efforts to reform the civil justice system have gone nowhere.

The political challenges are daunting. But if the community of insurance buyers becomes sufficiently motivated, it will eventually bring enough pressure to achieve systemic change. The balance of this chapter will provide a guide for legal reforms that are fair both to injured people and to insurance customers.

No-Fault Insurance

No discussion of reform of the legal system governing auto accident claims can begin without an analysis of the most widely debated subject, no-fault auto insurance. No-fault has been the centerpiece of two decades of debate, experimentation, criticism, study, controversy, and political struggle over how to control auto insurance cost.

As we have seen, the traditional liability system bases all awards for compensation on a determination of who is "at fault." The system seeks to make the "guilty" party pay. In the absence of agreement on fault, the legal system makes that determination. In a no-fault system, driver fault does not play a role in deciding who pays. Those injured in auto accidents are guaranteed payment from their own insurance company regardless of who is at fault.

As a shift away from traditional fault-based liability systems, genuine no-fault is most simply described as a trade-off. To cut the legal overhead costs, the no-fault policyholders give up the right to sue in most accident situations and accept certain limits on noneconomic damages. In return for those changes, the policyholder is guaranteed specified benefits, to be paid by his own insurance company, regardless of who caused the accident. No one worries who was how much at fault before paying the medical bills, lost wages, and other expenses of those injured. Each claimant looks to his own insurance for payment. The purpose of this system is to cut legal expenses, simplify getting money to injured people, get benefits to more people, and speed the whole process up.

For the community of insurance buyers as a whole, no-fault provides a simpler, quicker, and more efficient method of delivering compensation to people involved in vehicle accidents. In return for abandoning the traditional system of holding the guilty driver's insurance company responsible for paying the claim, insurance buyers get lower total costs, lower legal overhead, quicker payments, and no uncertainty about being paid. And the person who causes the accident or injury is still subject to criminal penalties and motor vehicle record sanctions.

The key criticism of the no-fault concept, other than the arguments coming from trial lawyers, is that it does not hold the person who caused the accident responsible for the injuries and damage caused to others. No-fault, critics charge, represents a complete uprooting of the traditional legal concept that everyone must be held responsible for his own actions.

We must not gloss over this difference. It is a fundamental trade-off between the practical and economic needs of the large group of insurance buyers and the moral imperative of holding people responsible for their actions. But as we already noted, the traditional liability system is not a very effective way to penalize bad driving or to deter future accident-causing behavior. In addition, since so few accidents are the sole fault of one driver, the effort to prove fault and force compensation based upon that decision is largely wasted. No-fault advocates therefore find the benefits of lower legal overhead, guaranteed benefits, and a simplified claims process to be much stronger than the moral imperative of punishment for wrongdoers.

No-fault is actually a misnomer. A more accurate description of the underlying philosophy of no-fault insurance laws is the phrase, "the assumption that the accident was no one's sole fault." This does not imply that someone is absolved from responsibility or that no blame can be attributed to the behavior that led to the accident. The assumption merely indicates that claims payments will be made without weighing how much each driver erred. It recognizes the fact that cars run into each other on our roads and highways and that accidents are rarely the result of a single act by one driver. Many accidents are caused by factors not related to either driver—bad roads, poor signs, foul weather, and pedestrian error. No-fault attempts to eliminate the unproductive and expensive fight over who has to pay how much. (Later in this chapter, we will consider an alternative name for "no-fault," in an effort to establish an accurate title for that type of system.)

A true no-fault system is a "cost-of-society" approach to compensating accident victims, recognizing that accidents are an unavoidable fact and establishing in advance simple rules for the process of paying for the costs of those accidents. The other simple rule of no-fault is that those who want to get paid must buy insurance. Each driver buys no-fault auto insurance in the same way as he does any other kind of insurance—for his own needs.

No-fault is appealing because it tackles the job of removing the economic incentives of lawyers in the auto claims system by removing them from the process. This explains the intense and emotional opposition of trial lawyers to no-fault. Because trial lawyers have been successful in weakening no-fault laws in practice, these laws have generally been a complex and confusing mixture of both the traditional liability system and the no-fault system, sometimes with disastrous results.

State to State

Up to this point we have looked at the auto insurance system, its costs, and where the premium dollar goes in the aggregate for the entire country. Now a comparison of various states' experiments with no-fault laws will illuminate the best and the worst.

The legislative push for no-fault began in the early 1970s. By 1976, fourteen states had adopted some form of a no-fault law, although none of these was a pure no-fault law: that is, none completely eliminated the right to sue. In fact, a pure no-fault law has never been enacted. Since none of them entirely eliminates the threat of suit, all of them contain both traditional liability and no-fault concepts. A vehicle owner must therefore buy the no-fault coverages for his own injuries and those of his passengers *in addition to* liability insurance to protect himself from the residual exposure to a lawsuit. The effectiveness of any particular no-fault law in keeping costs down is directly related to how tightly the law limits access to the traditional liability system and to the level of benefits provided by the no-fault law. Since no-fault benefits are guaranteed and will be paid regardless of any other factors, the use of the lawsuit system in addition to no-fault benefits actually increases costs beyond those of the traditional liability system alone. The easier it is to sue, the more expensive the claims process is and the more the cost-cutting purpose of the reform law is defeated. When both no-fault benefits and the lawsuit system are available, costs are much higher. Not only is the objective of lower legal overhead unfulfilled, but the opposite effect occurs—overall claims costs increase.

Any reform law that provides the best feature of no-fault—mandatory benefits paid by the driver's own insurance company—without limiting the right to file a lawsuit is improperly called "no-fault." Since these laws actually add opportunities for lawyers to exploit the system, they are referred to as "add-on" no-fault. These add-on states allow claimants to collect the guaranteed benefits of no-fault and then to sue for benefits in the traditional liability system.

The most cost-effective no-fault laws are those that clearly restrict the use of the lawsuit system and limit claims for non-economic damages. Lawsuit restrictions come in several forms. In Colorado, the injured person's losses must reach $2,500 before he can step into the lawsuit system. In Minnesota, the economic threshold is $4,000; in Connecticut, it is only $400. No one injured in an accident would have much difficulty reaching medical bills of $400. Several visits to a physician and one lab test would easily reach that amount. Entry into the lawsuit system is therefore not deterred at all by a law that sets such a low limit. Indeed, in practice these monetary thresholds establish a target for the injured person to reach, actually encouraging higher economic claims so the door to the lawsuit system can be opened. These monetary thresholds vary widely, accounting for wide differences in the effectiveness of the laws.

Several states have experimented with other types of thresholds; these are called "verbal thresholds" because they describe the types of injuries and situations that allow entry into the lawsuit system. In Michigan, for example, the verbal threshold specifies that a person must suffer serious injury, described as "serious impairment of bodily function, or permanent serious disfigurement, or death." If the injuries do not meet this qualification, then the injured person must collect his medical expenses and lost wages from his own insurance company under his no-fault policy and cannot file a lawsuit.

States also vary in the amount of no-fault benefits that insurance buyers are required to purchase. Hawaii requires a package totaling $15,000, New York sets a minimum of $50,000, and Michigan benefits start at $70,000. The higher the minimum amount required, the higher the cost to policyholders. In states with low minimum requirements, policyholders may purchase more insurance for their security, based on their needs.

For add-on states, those with both no-fault benefits and easy access to the lawsuit system, the results have been costly. Pennsylvania enacted a law requiring that injured persons are to be paid unlimited medical benefits from their no-fault coverage but then allowing the injured person to sue for more as soon as those medical expenses exceed $750. Many accident victims have collected both no-fault benefits and the proceeds of lawsuits. Premiums rose more than 20 percent per year to meet these spiraling and duplicative claims costs, with a predictable uproar from insurance buyers. Unable to overcome the opposition from trial lawyers, however, the Pennsylvania legislature enacted no reform of the system. In fact, in 1984, even the $750 threshold was eliminated, leaving the state with no restrictions on the use of the legal system. Now one of the worst insurance-crisis states, Pennsylvania has begun experimenting with new laws designed to cut rates in exchange for certain reforms.

New Jersey is the other notable example of the failure of add-on no-fault to deliver savings to insurance buyers. The New Jersey law was enacted with a mere $200 monetary threshold for medical expense before entry into the lawsuit system, in addition to payment of unlimited medical benefits under the no-fault policy. The lawsuit system continued unchanged, while costs doubled. As described in Chapter 4, New Jersey eventually established its Joint Underwriting Authority to meet consumers' demands for lower premiums. Without reducing underlying costs, the New Jersey system charged inadequate premiums and ran a deficit of $3 billion by 1989. The state's elected leadership abandoned the JUA system in response to consumer revolt over the surcharges they were required to pay to cover the JUA deficits. After all that trouble, New Jersey has still not come to grips with the costly nature of its add-on system of paying auto accident claims. For years it has had the highest or second highest auto insurance rates in the nation. Massachusetts is another state where a low monetary threshold, $500 until 1989, did little to hold down costs. Now, the threshold in Massachusetts is $2,000. In 1987 and 1988, Massachusetts passed New Jersey as the state with the highest insurance rates in the country.

A monetary threshold undermines the aim of lowering costs. Whether the limit is low or high, it provides an incentive for the injured person to reach that level of medical expenses to enter the lawsuit system. The role of lawyers in these systems is easy to understand: they encourage clients to reach the threshold so they will have an injury case to pursue. Monetary thresholds invite abuse of the no-fault benefits side of the claims system, driving costs in the wrong direction. All the costs of the traditional liability system, then, remain in place, in addition to the cost of guaranteed no-fault benefits. The cost of premiums soars.

New York's experience tells a different story. There, the original no-fault law included a $500 monetary threshold. When insurance customers experienced the same dramatic premium increases as in other add-on states, the New York legislature was successful in changing the law. In 1977, the monetary threshold was replaced with a verbal threshold describing the circumstances under which an injured person could file a suit. The new law also limited the fees doctors and hospitals could charge, thus capping medical payments. Lawsuit filings dropped off dramatically. For the next ten years New York policyholders experienced insurance rate increases lower than the rate of inflation. The New York State Insurance Department published a report indicating that overall auto insurance rates increased during that ten years by 42 percent, while the consumer price index rose by 80 percent.

The flurry of legislative activity in the early 1970s that led to the enactment of no-fault laws in some states was spurred on by a U.S. Department of Transportation study of auto insurance in the 1960s. That study found the traditional liability system to be ineffective, overly costly, and slow. For most states that have never adopted any type of no-fault law, that traditional lawsuit

FIGURE 5.2

Comparison of Auto Insurance Premium Increases by State, 1982–88

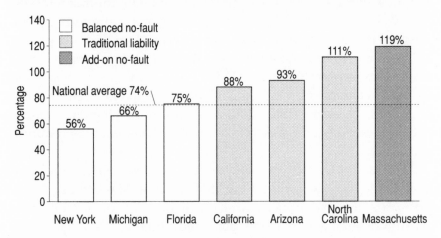

SOURCE: Best's Insurance Management Reports, Property/Casualty Release No. 4, February 5, 1990.

system is still in effect, and still costly and slow. California is its most notable example. In that state, insurance rates are the third-highest in the nation, behind New Jersey and Massachusetts. Consumers in California clearly indicated their rage at high auto insurance costs by enacting Proposition 103.

For comparison purposes, we will refer to states that effectively limit entrance to the lawsuit system as "balanced" no-fault states—guaranteed no-fault benefit costs have been balanced against lower legal expenses. As already discussed, states with low monetary thresholds or no lawsuit restrictions are add-on no-fault states. All other states have traditional liability systems. New York, Michigan, and Florida have balanced no-fault, while New Jersey and Massachusetts were both add-on states at the time the data in the studies cited in this chapter were compiled. California, Arizona, and North Carolina are traditional liability states. Figure 5.2 compares these three types of states.

California and New York offer a good comparison: they are states of similar size, with major urban centers, and similar costs of living. Best's list of average auto premiums by state for 1988 includes an analysis of premium growth from 1982 to 1988. For

New York, that increase was 56 percent over five years; for California, the increase was 88 percent during the same period. The national average was 74 percent. New York's premium increases fell well below other states, while California ran ahead of the average increase. This finding supports the New York Insurance Department report demonstrating that the state's balanced no-fault law has had the intended effect of controlling the increases in auto accident claims costs and the consequent premium increases. At the same time, California's traditional liability system has subjected insurance buyers to greater-than-average premium increases.

During that same five-year period, Florida experienced close-to-average increases amounting to 75 percent. Massachusetts, an add-on state, experienced an overall increase of 119 percent. North Carolina and Arizona, both traditional liability states, experienced increases of 111 percent and 93 percent, respectively. Michigan, a balanced no-fault state, had a below-average increase of 66 percent.

Of the seventeen states that by 1988 had some form of add-on no-fault or very low monetary threshold, eleven had greater-than-average premium increases from 1982 to 1988, two were right at the average, and four were slightly below average. None of the add-on states fell very far below the national average five-year premium increase.

Of nine states with balanced no-fault, including some form of verbal threshold or a high monetary threshold, seven were below the average increases and the other two were right at the average. None of the balanced no-fault states experienced higher-than-average premium increases during that period.

Of the traditional liability states, five were far over the average: Rhode Island, North Carolina, California, Arizona, and New Mexico. Several liability states were far below the average, including Iowa, West Virginia, Alabama, Nebraska, and Wyoming. But of the five states just listed with among the lowest auto insurance premium increases from 1982 to 1988, all had lower-than-average involvement of attorneys in auto accident claims. At the other end of the scale, four of the five liability states with the highest percentage increases also had higher-than-average involvement of attorneys. This statistic reconfirms the connection between increases in the cost of auto accident claims and the involvement of lawyers. Those states with the lowest percentage premium increases also rely less on the lawsuit system in a comparison of traditional liability states.

What then can we conclude from all this? No-fault can answer the need for lower legal overhead in auto insurance claims, but *only* if it is balanced—that is, only if the guaranteed benefits of no-fault policies are balanced with effective limits on use of the lawsuit system and limits on noneconomic damages. Experiments with no-fault added to the traditional lawsuit system cost more than leaving the traditional system alone. If anyone advocates no-fault as a means of controlling costs, he must advocate tough, balanced no-fault. Moreover, politicians who think they can enact real reform without cutting access to the lawsuit system are actually guaranteeing their constituents premium increases.

In addition to cutting legal overhead in auto accident claims, a tough and balanced no-fault law also solves other problems and provides additional benefits for insurance customers, claimants, and insurers.

A strong no-fault law eliminates the worry about being in an accident with an uninsured driver. Currently each consumer buying auto insurance in a traditional liability state will purchase uninsured motorist coverage. This UM part of the policy has become increasingly costly as the cost of auto accident claims has risen, particularly in areas with many uninsured drivers. Insurance customers are paying not only for their own insurance coverages but also against the risk of being involved in an accident with an uninsured driver. Under no-fault, since each driver looks to his own insurance for payment, the uninsured motorist portion of the policy is dramatically reduced. Except in the most serious accidents, the uninsured driver cannot collect from the insured driver's insurance policy. No-fault provides a strong incentive to buy at least minimal insurance, since the driver is prohibited from collecting from someone else. This arrangement reduces the drain on everyone's premium caused by the uninsured driver.

At present, the uninsured driver with no assets to protect has no incentive to buy auto insurance. In fact, he may be completely unable to afford insurance or to be financially responsible to another driver for injuries he may cause. The weakness of the liability system for a low-income driver is threefold. First, the liability system requires the low-income driver to be financially responsible for losses of others who may have much greater financial assets than he has. Second, if the low-income driver purchases liability insurance, he has protected himself from liability for other people's losses, but that insurance premium does nothing to protect him from loss of his car or for his own medical bills. Third, he has no incentive to protect other people on his limited budget; he needs every dollar he makes for his own needs, including food and shelter for his family. Insurance for other people is a very unfair use of his income. For low-income people living in metropolitan centers where average premiums are very high, the affordability problem is acute. That, in turn, causes higher numbers of uninsured drivers.

No-fault insurance for drivers having trouble affording auto insurance does two things. First, it relieves them from the obligation to purchase insurance for someone else's losses. Why should the man driving an old Ford, just barely making enough to feed and house his family, buy auto liability insurance so that if he hits someone driving a Cadillac the other driver will be taken care of? This is hardly fair. Under no-fault, except in the most serious accidents, the driver of the Cadillac will look to his own insurance company for compensation. Second, whatever money the low-income driver does spend to purchase no-fault coverage he will spend for his own benefit. It will protect him when he is injured, a protection that he would otherwise not have at all.

Insurance reform advocates use the word "equity" frequently in referring to the need for change in the auto insurance system. Surely, nothing can be less fair than requiring a low-income person to protect the assets of a higher-income person. Under a balanced no-fault system, the man driving the old Ford does not purchase insurance to protect other people's assets, so the person with many assets to protect pays to protect those assets. Each insurance buyer is able to select an amount of no-fault insurance above the minimum required by the law to suit his own economic needs and willingness to take risk.

No one knows when he gets into his car whether he will run into a Volkswagen or a Rolls Royce. No one knows in advance whether he will cause minimal injuries or very serious ones. No one can ever know how much liability insurance to buy to protect himself from hurting others. But consumers can choose how much protection to buy for themselves, based on their own needs, risks, and ability to afford. Under no-fault, fairness is served by forcing the driver with a lot to protect to pay for that extra protection. No-fault thus removes a source of the economic uncertainties that are part of the lawsuit lottery system.

An interesting quirk of no-fault laws has been that they are generally applied only to bodily injury claims and losses. Liability for damage to cars or other property is generally not included in the no-fault law. Only Michigan prohibits car owners from suing the other driver for vehicle damage as well as for injuries. Car owners there must rely on their own collision insurance to protect their cars. If we accept the notion that one of the risks of owning a car is that it may be damaged while being used, then we can probably accept the idea that the person owning the car should take care to insure it. We would never expect our next-door neighbor to share the cost of our homeowners' insurance, even though a fire in his house could consume both our houses. Our home is our own property and our worry to protect from loss. The automobile is an important physical asset owned by millions of Americans. Each owner should be expected to protect his property, according to its value, his ability to insure it, and his willingness to risk its loss.

In a pure no-fault system, each car owner would protect the physical value of his own car. Liability insurance for physical damage should be used to pay for damage to all property other than cars that may be damaged through someone's use of a car. If someone runs over his neighbor's fence, his auto property damage liability should pay for that damage. Throwing physical damage claims into the lawsuit system while bodily injury claims are handled through a no-fault payment system simply makes the costs higher for everyone. No-fault property damage for cars should be on the reform agenda, too.

Since no-fault provides a nonadversarial mechanism for handling claims, it cuts down on the time required to settle by eliminating a lot of the disputes that cause delays. No-fault benefits are paid more quickly to those who are injured than under the traditional liability system, where almost half of all injury claims are not settled a year after the accident. Moreover, the benefits that will be paid are specified in advance and guaranteed. The injured person does not have to worry about whether the other person will pay or whether he has insurance, nor does the injured person have to fight someone else's insurance company for payment. No-fault removes the risk that someone might not be paid at all.

In contrast, a risk-free lawsuit does not exist. Even after the wrangling and delay, a judge or jury could decide that a person was partly at fault and entitled only to part of his damages from the other driver's insurance. The hiring of a lawyer or the filing of a lawsuit does not guarantee payment. In addition, the lawsuit system is slow. The injured person could go for months or years not knowing if he will be reimbursed for his medical bills. That delay and uncertainty are eliminated with no-fault insurance, along with the confusion or argument over who will pay, what benefits, and when.

Finally, no-fault has a very beneficial cost-cutting side effect that has nothing to do with the lawsuit system. No-fault discourages false, fraudulent, and inflated claims. Under this system, it is far more difficult for a claimant to file duplicate claims, claims for nonexistent injuries, or grossly inflated claims with his own insurance company. If he does, the claim file soon stands out, and the insurance company can stop the fraud. Serious auto insurance fraud schemes, such as staged auto accidents, would be very difficult to sustain under a strong no-fault law. Since the fraud criminal relies on taking money from someone else's liability insurance policy, a strong no-fault law hurts his business. Fraudulent abuse of the insurance claims dollar would be cut dramatically.

No-fault insurance, by allowing insurance companies and their customers a closer relationship in claims resolutions and by eliminating a lot of contact between a claimant and the other person's insurance company, creates a closer partnership between insurer and insured. Individuals will be more concerned about their own claims record and much less likely to inflate or pad a claim they are filing with their own company. A person's claims record becomes as important as his driving record, giving him an incentive to control claims costs rather than increase them. No-fault uses the self-interest of insurance customers to control costs. The perverse incentive of the traditional liability system, to build up claims, is reversed. The insurance claims lottery, with its disproportionate enrichment to some claimants, is also eliminated.

Criticism of No-Fault

No-fault insurance, however, has its critics. The loudest criticism of no-fault has been that it fails to cut costs. Several studies examining all the states where no-fault has been enacted, both balanced and add-on, have concluded that no-fault does not save money for policyholders. As we saw earlier, though, there are many kinds of no-fault laws in effect around the country. All the benefits of no-fault insurance can be gained by simply enacting a law that guarantees insurance benefits, under which people will seek payment first from their own insurance company. Without tight restrictions on the use of the lawsuit system and limits on noneconomic damages, however, insurance buyers will not benefit. In fact, if no-fault is added on to an existing liability system, rates go up faster. Only tough, balanced no-fault will deliver cost control for insurance buyers. (Under any system, of course, rates will go up to reflect increases in the cost of medical care and car repairs.)

One argument regularly voiced in opposition to no-fault, particularly by trial lawyers, is that it lets bad drivers off the hook, thus rewarding irresponsibility. In fact, it does not do this. All drivers still have their claims record and their driver's license to be concerned about. The driver who regularly causes accidents will soon find his insurance rates skyrocketing. No-fault rewards people for being cautious and avoiding accidents, even those that would have been someone else's fault.

Another criticism is that no-fault turns its back on people who are seriously hurt. But even in balanced no-fault states, each driver is subject to being sued for causing serious and permanent injury to another person. Drivers who purchase no-fault insurance for themselves also purchase "residual" liability coverage against the possibility that they may be sued over a very serious accident. The intent of no-fault insurance is to take care of the 90 percent of accidents that do not involve serious and permanent injuries, disfigurement, or death. Even the toughest no-fault insurance law allows suits in these serious accidents. The other key exception to the restriction against lawsuits is for cases where the person causing the accident was grossly negligent, careless of the well-being of others, or reckless. This category would include drunk or drugged drivers as well as those using excessive speed or committing other gross recklessness. These drivers would not be immune to lawsuits by those they injure. The civil justice system would function in its intended way to hold these individuals responsible for their behavior. In some of these situations, the criminal justice system may be used as well to punish the wrongdoer.

The one criticism that lingers is that a no-fault insurance system is unfair to the innocent driver who does not have serious injuries, is not hit by a grossly negligent driver, and must seek compensation from his own insurance company. In this situation the driver's accident was clearly not his fault. He must make a claim with his own insurance company for his medical bills, even though the other driver broke a traffic law and caused the crash. The other driver's insurance does not pay for the innocent driver's losses, and, from a purely economic point of view, the at-fault driver is not held responsible.

The only consolation for the innocent driver in this circumstance is that he does not have to worry about where the money will come from to pay his losses, and he does not have to wait long to be paid. Undoubtedly, of course, each driver who finds himself in this situation will feel that the system has a quirk of unfairness in it. Even good drivers have accidents. Each person who considers whether a no-fault system is a better alternative than the traditional liability system for handling auto accident claims must either accept or reject one fact in general. The choice between a traditional liability system and a balanced no-fault system must be made with full knowledge of the trade-offs: every attempt to soften those trade-offs by retaining the lawsuit system in addition to a no-fault benefits system leads to higher premiums for consumers.

How people assess these trade-offs is an interesting issue. In October 1990, the Gallup Organization released the results of a poll taken from telephone interviews with 1,500 U.S. households in May and June 1990. The results showed that more than 80 percent of car owners agreed that it would be a good idea if injured people could get paid by their own auto insurers instead of having to file claims against the other driver. More than 85 percent said they were willing to restrict payments to actual medical expenses and lost wages in minor injury accidents and to prohibit claims or lawsuits against the other driver unless injuries were serious or permanent. Sixty-eight percent of those interviewed said they would be willing to prohibit all lawsuits if those with serious or permanent injuries were offered some compensation over and above their medical expenses and lost wages. The survey found that 78 percent of the public favors giving car owners a choice of buying auto insurance that pays without regard to fault or one that requires a fault determination. The survey also checked how people would feel about a law like Michigan's that would prohibit suits for damage to cars; 84 percent of the survey respondents thought that was a good idea.

No-fault has had mixed success over the past two decades in states around the country because passing laws requires compromise. Legislators juggle the demands of insurance companies, consumers, lawyers, doctors, and auto repair firms in the process of enacting legislation to reform insurance. In many cases compromise has resulted in unbalanced no-fault. That compromise has led to a long list of states that consider no-fault legislation a failure. That failure proceeds directly from laws that did not squarely face the need for real trade-offs, for restrictions on the filing of lawsuits and limits on noneconomic damages in exchange for guaranteed no-fault benefits.

Politicians are especially vulnerable to the criticism of trial lawyers that no-fault would take away someone's right to sue, especially if that person has been injured. The political environment does not allow them to restrict rights; instead, a politician must be a valiant protector of rights. This has made balanced no-fault an easy target for defeat in the political arena.

Some intriguing alternative proposals are making the rounds currently, including one called "choice no-fault." This proposal has been enacted in several states, but it is too early to see the results. Choice no-fault would, for example, allow each car owner to choose between a no-fault policy, with restrictions on the right to sue, and a traditional liability policy, the no-fault policy being cheaper than the liability policy. The system is complex because all kinds of mechanisms have to be set up to take care of the situations when a no-fault policyholder and a traditional liability policyholder collide. The idea has some advocates in the political debate, however, because it relieves the legislator from responsibility for taking away someone's rights. The consumer can choose.

One other important note on the public and political debate over no-fault should be considered: discarding the term "no-fault." The term does not accurately describe what a no-fault insurance policy does for the policyholder. The name in use in some no-fault states is "personal injury protection," sometimes indicated with the acronym PIP. Something new is needed, though, that reflects the most important features of a balanced no-fault system—that benefits are guaranteed, that claims will be paid quickly without hassle, and that each car owner assumes responsibility for insuring his own risks. Auto insurance under no-fault is more like homeowner's insurance; that is, the individual is buying coverage to protect himself from economic misfortune. "Guaranteed benefits auto insurance" is a better term for a balanced no-fault system.

This detailed discussion of no-fault is important because guaranteed benefits auto insurance holds the most promise for reversing some of the perverse cost-increasing incentives in the claims system, for cutting direct legal costs, and for eliminating a lot of abuse. The states have experimented with many cost-reduction schemes, providing us with an opportunity to see the results of different laws. The guaranteed benefits solution has been on the table for more than twenty years: it simply needs to be implemented without being diluted.

Other Legal Reforms

Before closing this chapter, we should touch on some other concepts that have been debated from time to time as alternatives for cutting the legal overhead of the auto insurance claims system. Six ideas are worth a quick look: caps on damage awards, penalties for nonmeritorious suits, mandatory arbitration of disputes, elimination of lawsuit procedures, elimination of jury trials, and elimination of the collateral source rule.

Caps, or limits, on damage awards have been used to control the amount paid for certain claims. Limits on damage awards are most appropriately used on noneconomic damages. Limits on economic damages can be harmful when a person's actual injuries are very serious, requiring complicated and lengthy medical treatment; a $250,000 cap on economic damages would be devastatingly unfair to a person whose medical bills amounted to $500,000. Most often, legislators choose to limit the amount that may be awarded over and above actual economic damages, for emotional damages such as pain and suffering. Although these kinds of caps are effective in limiting the largest awards that may result from a verdict, they are not useful in cutting down the legal expense associated with the lawsuit system. They provide no deterrence to the filing of suits, do not affect the majority of smaller suits and awards, and do not serve as disincentives to build-up of economic losses.

The civil justice system currently provides few penalties for filing frivolous or nonmeritorious liability lawsuits. This is true for all types of lawsuits, not just auto accident cases. The defendant, who may be innocent or only partially responsible, is brought into court at his expense or that of his insurance company to defend against the charges made in the lawsuit. If he is vindicated through the legal process, he is unable to collect for the lost time, and the insurance company may not collect the legal expense of defending him. In the worst cases of abuse, the defendant has the option of countersuing for malicious prosecution, but in the vast number of cases the vindicated defendant and his insurer are still losers. If a system could be established allowing that person to be compensated for his time and legal expense for self-defense, fewer frivolous suits would be filed. Plaintiffs' attorneys would have to be very careful in selecting whom to sue.

Mandatory arbitration has been proposed for some types of liability as a way to determine more quickly who is liable to pay damages and how much. In this system both parties (or all parties if more than two) agree to have their case reviewed by a panel of judges (an arbitration panel) who will issue a decision. The arbitration panel serves as a sort of mini-court. Each party agrees in advance to be bound by the decision—thus the term "mandatory arbitration." The intent is to speed up the process of resolving the dispute over who must pay and how much. So far, however, little evidence exists to show that this type of system is any less expensive than the traditional legal route. Lawyers are still involved to represent each party, and the basic costs of the system, similar to the costs of the court system, must still be met.

Proposals to reduce the legal maneuvering through elimination or reform of procedural rules have generally been unsuccessful in cutting costs. In fact, much "legal reform" has actually led to more complicated procedures and more delays, rather than less. Efforts to speed up resolution of cases through laws requiring shorter time frames for certain parts of the lawsuit process have been met with greater numbers of letters among lawyers notifying each other of deadlines and requests for extensions and other paperwork. Procedural changes, it seems, do not lower legal overhead.

One legal reform advocate, Peter Huber, argues that trial by jury for most auto accident cases should be eliminated. He notes that the process of jury selection is exceedingly slow and does not lead to particularly good resolution of disputes. He advocates the use of jury trials only for the most serious civil liability and criminal trials, where the constitutional guarantee of "trial by a jury of peers" is warranted. The threat of trial by jury forces up the value of settlements, since few people who have injured someone else in an auto accident want to face a jury that will naturally be sympathetic to the injured party. But because most cases are settled in earlier phases of the lawsuit process, very few cases go all the way to trial anyway. The value of the settlement has already been driven up during the settlement process. Using a judge or panel of judges instead of a jury in those few cases that do go all the way to jury trial does nothing to eliminate the costs of lawyers, courts, or judges. And it would not, of course, do anything to reverse the cost-building incentives of the lawsuit system.

One change that would have a positive effect would be the elimination of the collateral source rule. This rule does not allow juries or judges to hear evidence or to take into account other sources of compensation an injured person may have in determining the amount of damages to award, resulting in an enormous amount of duplication in payments to claimants. Whether this rule is right or wrong can be debated, and the author makes no judgment about it. The fact is that its application in lawsuits causes insurance claims payments to be higher than what is required to make the injured person whole again financially. This legal rule costs money, and that money comes from all policyholders. The clash of rights is between the community of insurance buyers, who do not wish to overpay claimants out of the pool of premiums, and claimants, who expect to collect their full damages from all the sources of compensation possible. Even elimination of the collateral source rule, though, would not cut down the number of lawsuits, lessen the involvement of lawyers, or lower the direct legal overhead of the liability system.

As we have seen, the lawsuit system is an inefficient and uneconomical means of figuring out who pays how much after a car crash. Not only does the legal overhead cost a lot of money, but it drives the economic losses higher than necessary, in turn leading to higher multiples of noneconomic losses. The system provides all the wrong incentives for lowering costs and invites abuse and fraud.

This system does not serve the practical self-interest of insurance buyers. The alternative, guaranteed benefits auto insurance, must be put in place with tough trade-offs. While politically difficult to achieve, it is not impossible. If New York can enact balanced no-fault, creating guaranteed benefits auto insurance for its residents, surely other states can. New York's success is traceable to the passage of its law in the mid-1970s before the trial lawyers were prepared to defeat it. Any effort to enact balanced no-fault in the 1990s will have to overcome stiff opposition of trial lawyers who have a battle-hardened and successful formula for defeating any law that would legislate away their economic self-interest.

Although it is probably true that passing a law that would cut lawyers out of the system is impossible, legislating away the incentives for using lawyers is possible. If insurance buyers can be given incentives to avoid using the legal system—incentives that lower their costs—then we may still have a chance for real reform. That incentive is contained in a guarantee of benefits and in the lower costs brought about by less use of the lawsuit system. The need for change in the lawsuit system is urgent and critical to every insurance buyer.

Cutting Costs

C hapter 5 dealt with how to trim legal overhead, which affects primarily the bodily injury liability portion of the insurance policy. The auto insurance system, though, can be improved in many other ways. This chapter will look at other areas where claim dollars are paid and savings are possible. The discussion falls into three sections—preventive strategies, after-the-loss strategies, and information strategies.

While each of these proposals would help reduce or stabilize auto insurance premiums for insurance buyers, implementation of some of them may create costs of their own. To cite one example, if every automobile on the road were equipped with airbags to protect passengers from serious injuries in head-on collisions, auto insurance rates would be reduced, reflecting the lessened injury claims; the cost would be paid by consumers purchasing cars. We will point out these instances where savings in auto insurance may raise other costs to consumers, allowing readers to choose what makes most sense.

Preventive Strategies

Any effort that leads to fewer accidents, less severe accidents, less serious injuries, or less property damage will lower the cost of auto accident claims. Insurance buyers will benefit from such prevention strategies, as will those individuals whose injuries never occurred or were less severe because of some prevention or damage-mitigation program. Many states have enacted such laws, but much remains to be done.

Alcohol and drugs

Drivers impaired by alcohol or drugs are responsible for half of all highway fatalities in the United States. In 1987, for instance, drunk and drugged drivers caused more than 23,000 deaths and more than 500,000 injuries. Of those who died, almost half had a blood alcohol content high enough to be convicted of drunk driving under the laws of most states. The Insurance Information Institute concluded, "If only one thing could be changed about driving in America that would significantly affect the numbers of deaths and injuries on our nation's highways, the cost of insurance claims, and the price of auto insurance, it is the prevention of drunk driving." Further, the institute estimates that if there were even 10 percent fewer accidents caused by drunk or drugged drivers, there would be 2,400 fewer deaths, 70,000 fewer injuries, and over $1 billion in savings on insurance claims. While we cannot prevent every citizen who drinks too much from getting behind the wheel of an automobile, we have laws that, if enforced, will deter many from driving while impaired.

The public campaign to prevent drinking and driving took center stage in the early 1980s when Mothers Against Drunk Driving (MADD) and other citizen action groups focused attention on the problems associated with drunk driving. Their lobbying brought about changes in several key states. When Maine, for example, enacted a strict law in 1981, traffic fatalities fell there by 40 percent. This success brought national attention to the campaign for stronger laws to deter drunk driving. In 1984, the federal government passed a law that would withhold highway funding from states that did not raise their drinking age to twenty-one. By 1988, all states had raised their minimum drinking age to twenty-one. Since 1983, driving-while-intoxicated arrest rates have declined 14 percent for drivers in the eighteen to twenty age range, reflecting this increase in the legal drinking age across the country.

Most states have also enacted laws that define legal intoxication. This threshold, known as blood alcohol concentration (BAC), is expressed as a percentage of the chemical alcohol in the blood. In most states this percentage is 0.10. According to the American Medical Association (AMA), the probability of an impaired driver being in an accident increases sharply at 0.05 percent, half the legal BAC for most states. Under 0.05 percent, the probability of causing an auto accident is about the same as a sober person. In 1985 the AMA recommended that 0.05 percent BAC be adopted as the legal limit for drivers. For a person weighing around 120 pounds, two drinks in a period of two hours would exceed the 0.05 percent level; for a 200-pound person, three drinks in two hours would pass that limit.

Public perception of the problem of drinking and driving is important to preventive efforts. During the past decade of national attention on the issue, public attitudes against drunk driving have hardened. Awareness of the social costs has changed the behavior of many drinkers. Recently, however, the media has not treated drunk driving as a front-burner issue. According to a report by the Insurance Information Institute, the Harvard School of Public Health concluded that media coverage of the drunk-driving problem peaked in 1984 and has declined since then.

Much has been accomplished, even if media attention has eased. Clearly the issue was driven to the forefront of legislative and public debate by the emotional and social costs of the loss of life from drunk-driving accidents, articulated by MADD and other groups. Those efforts resulted in stricter laws, stiffer penalties, and a shift in public opinion. The job is not finished, however. Efforts to prevent drunk driving need new momentum, a momentum that can be generated only by insurance buyers who are paying for the huge economic losses caused by alcohol- and drug-impaired drivers.

This summary of proposals from various institutes, associations, and government agencies illustrates ways to attack the problem:

- Lower the legal blood alcohol content (BAC) level. Most states now set the limit at 0.10 percent. While some states have lowered their legal limit to 0.08 percent, the AMA recommends 0.05 percent. The closer to the AMA standard, the greater will be the deterrent effect.

- Enact laws authorizing a longer suspension or even a revocation of a driver's license if an individual is found by law enforcement to be driving with a BAC above the legal limit. These laws are sometimes called administrative or automatic license revocation statutes.

- Establish mandatory fines for drunk-driving offenses that are high enough to be a deterrent and that cannot be softened (in other words, plea bargained by a lawyer) under any circumstances.

- Enforce the Commercial Motor Vehicle Safety Act of 1986 that created stronger licensing, testing, and other standards for heavy truck operators, including a 0.04 percent BAC, which are to be enacted and enforced through state laws.

- Enact laws permitting authorities to confiscate and impound cars of repeat offenders and dangerous drivers; or require installation of ignition interlock devices preventing driving while intoxicated.

- Use more visible enforcement and detection programs such as roadblocks or sobriety checkpoints.

- Authorize law-enforcement officials to use preliminary breath testing devices at roadside to deter drunk driving and to improve the quality of arrests.

- Increase media coverage and public awareness of programs designed to detect and arrest impaired drivers, increasing public perception of the probability of being caught.

Research has shown that if people believe that the likelihood of being caught is great and that the penalty will be applied surely and swiftly, that knowledge is a strong deterrent. Stronger penalties for repeat offenders are important but do not necessarily result in modified behavior. For most drivers, the threat of being caught and punished immediately through automatic license suspension is the most effective deterrent. This preventive concept is showing better results than after-the-fact penalties and is less costly to law enforcement and the judicial system.

The prevention of accidents caused by alcohol- and drug-impaired drivers will have the greatest impact of any prevention strategy on auto accident claims costs and on the premiums paid by insurance buyers. It deserves our highest priority and greatest effort and allocation of resources: success at preventing impaired driving will pay the greatest rewards.

Vehicle, highway, and driver safety

Perhaps the next most important area for preventing accidents is safety—vehicle safety, highway and road safety, and driver safety.

Vehicle design is closely related to the cost of insurance. In a larger car, for example, injuries will be far less severe than in a small car. Although small, fuel-efficient cars are here to stay, features that can lessen injuries in accidents can be made standard in any vehicle. Some of these features are airbags, side-impact restraints, antilock brakes, and other safety technology. The National Highway Traffic Safety Administration estimates that if all cars were equipped with airbags and if at least half of all front-seat passengers wore lap/shoulder seatbelts in addition to having airbags, the number of deaths and critical injuries prevented would be twice that of the belts alone, saving 9,000 lives per year. The National Highway Traffic Safety Administration, which has focused attention on the safety value of airbags in head-on collisions, is also studying side-impact collisions and has unveiled new requirements for car design that will further protect passengers from injury in this type of collision. The initial investment in airbags, side-impact restraints, and other safety features may seem high to the car buyer, but the savings in lives and accident costs will be considerable in the long run. The installation and use of these devices should be promoted.

Vehicle design is also an important factor in the cost of repairing the car. Different types of cars and different manufacturing techniques have a direct impact on the cost of car repair after an accident. Design features such as damage-resistant bumpers and easily replaceable body parts diminish the extent of damage and the cost to repair the car. A recent study by the Insurance Research Council based on a Roper Organization, Inc., survey shows that 70 percent of Americans think car bumpers are too weak and that the federal standard for damage-resistant bumpers should be increased. Other features, such as unibody construction, raise repair costs. All such repair costs are reported in comparisons of "repairability" and collision losses compiled by the Highway Loss Data Institute.

One way insurance buyers would benefit is if the information about safety and repairability is made available to consumers at the time they are considering buying an automobile, since these factors will be reflected in the costs of insuring a car. Almost all insurers provide discounts in their rating plans for cars with better-than-average "repairability" figures through the use of make-and-model rating plans, which categorize each car based on actual performance. This rating system has brought about a very healthy dialogue between insurers and car manufacturers on ways to reduce the damageability of cars during the design phase, and provides car makers with a marketplace motivation for reaching higher repairability standards. The only problem for consumers is that when these repairability discounts are built into the rating system, they are hidden. No simple damageability rating system is available when the consumer buys the car.

Consumers should be able to compare cars they are considering buying with information about safety features, repairability, and insurance analyses. Consumers should have two ways to get this information—either through insurance company publication of "car guides" or through federal government requirements on new car sales. Either way, manufacturers would be forced to compete for car buyers based on ratings for safety, repairability, theft prevention, and other design features that directly affect insurance costs.

Governments play an important role in highway and road safety, so they must be considered in any plan to reduce auto insurance costs. This role ranges from the actual design and building of roads to the enactment and enforcement of all traffic laws. States enact laws governing every aspect of the rules of the road—laws on right of way, mandatory seatbelt or motorcycle helmet use, lights and signs, lane markings and rules, pedestrian and bicycle rights, registration and operation of vehicles, driver behavior, speed limits and zones, and penalties for breaking traffic laws. The federal government has been closely involved in setting rules for America's highways through the Department of Transportation, governing speed limits, interstate trucking, and auto safety and design.

Rigorous enforcement of all existing traffic control and safety laws would change driving behavior, making driving, riding, and walking less hazardous—and result in substantially fewer injuries, deaths, and economic losses on our roads and highways. Insurance costs would therefore be less. Of course, increased enforcement does entail a greater allocation of government resources, which is often not an option because of government budget priorities. Laws and safety requirements vary from state to state, and some states have enacted additional laws that promote greater highway and vehicle safety. Some of the proposals worth pursuing in all states include:

- enacting and enforcing mandatory seatbelt laws

- enacting child restraint or child safety-seat laws

- requiring motorcyclists to wear protective headgear

- strengthening speed limit laws; toughening speed violation penalties

- improving driver training programs, including retraining in target age groups; adding training on socially responsible driving, insurance costs, and the hazards of drunk driving

- promoting mature driver training programs, such as the "55 Alive" program sponsored by American Association of Retired Persons, that are rewarded by insurance discounts

- enacting "crash avoidance" traffic control laws such as repeal of right-turn-on-red rules at high-accident intersections

- enacting, strengthening, and enforcing all repeat offender laws

- strengthening the capabilities of motor vehicle departments to keep accurate driving history records, including data exchanges with other states

- eliminating programs that allow traffic law violators to erase or "mask" offenses from their driving records by attending traffic school

- banning use of radar detectors

- enacting regulations for truck safety inspections and truck operator training standards

- clearing highway and road shoulders to eliminate obstructions to vision and dangerous roadside hazards; installing breakaway supports for all roadside lights, fixtures, and signs; installing crash barriers

Each of these worthy suggestions has been proved to reduce the hazards of being on the road. Even if every one of them is enacted into law, however, enforcement is still the key, and this requires more government funding. Citizens and communities must set their own priorities for allocating law-enforcement resources and highway funds. More communities might be willing to take the necessary steps if they knew their efforts would result in lower accident costs. Insurers can help in determining this. Indeed, communities should consider the implications for insurance costs of their land use, development, and transportation system planning, especially for dense metropolitan areas where insurance costs are high because of more accidents and higher claims costs.

Preventing vehicle theft

The final loss-prevention effort we will discuss concerns vehicle theft. If we could better prevent cars from being stolen, we would save a huge amount of money. The trend in auto theft has been up dramatically since 1984: in that year, 1 million autos were stolen in the United States. By 1988, the number exceeded 1.4 million. Over the past two decades, recoveries of stolen vehicles have declined significantly. Whereas in 1960 nearly 90 percent of stolen vehicles were returned to their owners, now little more than half are returned. Law-enforcement officials attribute the decline in recovery of stolen cars to professional theft rings that steal and dismantle cars for profit or export them out of the United States. It is a serious organized criminal business. Over the last ten years, under 15 percent of all vehicle theft crimes have resulted in arrests.

The FBI estimates that losses related to vehicle thefts have risen to a staggering $8.4 billion a year. It is no coincidence that those states with the worst auto theft—California, Massachusetts, and New Jersey—also have the highest insurance rates in the nation. Insurance buyers in those states have the most reason to be concerned about the problem. Even a 10 or 20 percent decrease in the number of stolen cars would mean considerable savings for insurance buyers.

In 1984 President Reagan signed the Motor Vehicle Theft Law Enforcement Act. This law instituted three things. First, it required auto manufacturers to mark new autos with the vehicle identification number (VIN) on fourteen major car parts of particular models that have been shown to be likely theft targets. The fourteen car parts are those found most useful to "chop shops." This additional marking of car parts works as a deterrent, making it easier for law enforcement to trace cars and parts. Second, the act made it a felony to alter or remove vehicle identification numbers, providing a $10,000 fine and imprisonment of up to five years. Third, the act made it illegal to import or export stolen vehicles and gave customs officials special authority to inspect and enforce the law, providing a $15,000 fine and imprisonment for conviction.

Another important innovation has been the National Auto Theft Bureau's expansion of its ability to computerize nationwide information about stolen autos. Thieves often move cars and car parts across state lines to falsify registration and identification of vehicles. The bureau is now able to identify 255 million vehicles through on-line records and inform law enforcement and insurance companies on the validity of vehicle numbers and the location of impounded cars.

Massachusetts and south Florida have begun to experiment with a new device installed in cars to foil car thieves. Unlike the typical noisy car alarm that is only a minimally effective deterrent, these new devices are actually electronic tracking systems hooked into the police station. The owner installs the unit in the car in an inconspicuous place. If the car is stolen, the owner calls the police, who activate the homing unit. The unit in the car emits a signal so that police with special scanners can track the vehicle. Since 1986, with the units installed in 35,000 cars, more than 900 cars have been recovered, with a 95 percent success rate. Average recovery time is ninety minutes, and the arrest rate is higher than overall auto-theft arrest rates by 10 percent. This type of auto theft prevention is fairly expensive, however, since the police must have tracking devices and the individual car owners must buy their own transmitters. But it is clearly effective in getting the stolen property back before the thief has a chance to dismantle or sell it.

New Jersey is attacking its theft problem with a Combat Auto Theft (CAT) program. This new law permits local police chiefs to establish a car registration program in which citizens who do not normally drive between 1:00 A.M. and 5:00 A.M. voluntarily display a sticker on their cars. Police are authorized to stop any stickered vehicle they see on the streets during those hours. This CAT program is similar to one begun in 1987 in several New York City precincts, which has now been expanded statewide. A New York survey found that of nearly 18,000 autos registered and window stickered, only eighteen were stolen during a two-year period. This antitheft program, which allows car owners to deter the theft of their own cars, has had a dramatic effect on theft rates in New York City. Insurers are beginning to provide discounts on comprehensive coverage for their customers who display a CAT window decal.

One problem is that some auto thefts are not thefts at all, but rather schemes to defraud insurance companies. In October 1990 the *Wall Street Journal* reported on schemes designed to get money for "stolen" cars. The report opened with the story of a Dallas-area swimming hole that developed an oil slick. When police investigated the source of the oil, they found that the bottom of the pool, an abandoned stone quarry, was littered with twenty late-model cars, some of them brand new. All the vehicles had been reported stolen, and the insurers had already paid off the owners. In contrast to most claims reports, many still had the keys in the ignition, and none of them had been stripped of stereos, wheels, or other accessories. The police concluded that the cars had not been stolen but dumped by the owners for the insurance cash.

It is estimated that 25 percent of all vehicle theft claims involve some kind of insurance fraud. The vehicle owners themselves commit at least half this fraud by filing a theft claim with their insurance company for a vehicle they have disposed of one way or another. The owners then attempt to collect the insurance claim payment. Many people have become blasé about insurance fraud because they see it as a victimless crime. It is not, of course; we are the victims, insurance customers.

These steps should be taken to reverse the trend in auto theft and fraud:

- Enact tough legislation and penalties to deal with thieves, chop shop activity, and illegal export of stolen cars.

- Implement mandatory vehicle inspection and identification programs by insurance companies to detect "phantom" vehicles and those with phony or false documentation and to eliminate claims for preexisting damage.

- Create a special fraud bureau within each state insurance department with broad enforcement authority;

fund special programs within insurance departments to support law enforcement and prosecution initiatives.

- Establish within individual insurance companies special investigative units to detect fraud and investigate theft.

- Implement cooperative programs among insurance companies and local law enforcement in investigation and recovery of stolen vehicles.

- Use all available services of the National Auto Theft Bureau.

- Support local database development on the causes, locations, and times of theft within a community, which allows local law enforcement to use its resources to stop theft more effectively.

- Support international efforts to detect and stop exports of stolen autos from country to country, such as the International Association of Auto Theft Investigators, recently established by the leaders of antitheft bureaus from the United States, Canada, Sweden, France, and Holland.

- Require auto manufacturers to implement additional vehicle marking programs.

- Speed up cooperation among states to create uniform salvage and title laws to prevent "title-wash" from state to state.

- Create community-based crime watch groups and "hotline" programs to facilitate citizen participation in antitheft efforts, such as HEAT (Help Eliminate Auto Theft) programs in place in some states in which citizens call a toll-free hotline number to report information about stolen cars and receive an award if the tip leads to an arrest.

- Provide incentives to car owners to install antitheft devices.

- Establish CAT-type window decal programs to assist citizens and law enforcement in snagging stolen autos and deterring theft.

The point of all this is to save money for insurance buyers. Car thieves are picking the pockets of insurance customers every day. Preventing auto theft will directly benefit consumers.

To the extent that auto accidents and theft can be prevented, auto insurance claims will be reduced. Prevention may be expensive, but it is much cheaper than paying for theft and accidents through insurance—not to mention what it saves in human suffering. Prevention programs should have the highest priority among solutions proposed to the high cost of auto insurance.

After-the-Loss Strategies

If every prevention proposal is pursued vigorously, some auto accidents and claims will be avoided. We all know, however, that many autos will still bump into each other, and theft will continue. In this section, we will examine three simple proposals that, if implemented, would lower the cost of auto accident claims *after the loss:* elimination of duplicate payments, more competition in the auto repair and auto replacement parts business, and stronger prosecution of wrongdoers. But first we will examine one proposal commonly mentioned in discussions of cost control—medical cost containment.

Medical cost

In Chapter 2, we showed that only $10 out of every $100 in insurance revenue goes to pay for the medical care and expenses of people injured in automobile accidents. That amount is less than the amount paid to lawyers and the legal system and is also less than the amount paid for noneconomic damages.

That $10 pays for the doctor fees, hospital costs, emergency services, ambulances, surgeons, specialists, nurses' care, rehabilitation programs, special equipment, prescriptions, and all other expenses related to bringing injured people back to health. That $10 even includes the cost for funeral services for those killed in auto accidents, as well as death benefits for surviving family members. Although our highest human priority after an accident is providing medical attention for anyone who is hurt, medical care amounts to only 10 percent of the auto insurance dollar.

For all the discussion about the spiraling costs of health care, the amount of the auto insurance premiums going to medical expenses is not out of proportion to what is being delivered. The rest of the claims expenses related to injury claims *are* out of proportion: the dollars paid to lawyers and the amount paid for noneconomic damages. Overall medical care costs in this country have gone up faster than the rate of inflation in the past few years, contributing to increases in the cost of all kinds of insurance that provide medical benefits, not just automobile insurance. Health insurance, where the increases in medical costs are direct and immediate, has shown the most dramatic rise in costs. In auto insurance, though, where medical expenses are only $10 out of every $100 in insurance revenue and represent only 26 percent of all the money paid out in injury claims, medical expenses are not the worst of the problem. The most ambitious cost-containment program might trim a percentage point or two out of that figure, but the effort would result in only slight savings for the insurance buyer. In fact, the effort to cut those expenses could cost more than what would be saved.

Medical care expenses can, however, be trimmed directly through the auto insurance system in two ways. One is by exposing medical claims for nonexistent injuries, fraudulent claims, or other deliberate deceptions. Even if detecting and eliminating these payments cost as much as is saved, it is the morally right thing to do for insurance customers. Second, as explained earlier, the present system actually encourages people to increase their medical expenses and other costs of their injuries, to build up the claim, and get a larger payment for noneconomic damages, usually a multiple of actual economic damages. This perverse incentive will be reversed only when the claims-handling system ceases to reward cost building. The solution in this case is to remove the noneconomic rewards for most minor injury situations and get most claims out of the traditional lawsuit system. The cost of medical care, and its dramatic increases in recent years, is of great concern because the actual costs of caring for injured people drive the other costs for bodily injury claims: the build-up of economic losses, noneconomic damages, and legal expenses.

We cannot estimate how much of the insurance premium would be saved by eliminating payments for fraudulent claims and reversing the incentives to building up medical claims. Clearly, however, those two factors, fraud and build-up, are far more worthy of our attention than any effort to cut the cost of legitimate medical expenses for injured people. Debates about the cost of health care usually center around how to cut the fees paid to doctors or how to lower the average per day charge made by hospitals for patient care. This debate, at least for auto injury claims, will be unproductive and probably unfair to those unfortunate people injured in auto accidents who are legitimately entitled to the best medical care.

The discussion of containing health care costs should be left to other debates, like that over the cost of public and private health insurance. If those discussions provide any solutions to escalating medical costs, then naturally those same efficiencies should be used to lower medical costs wherever they occur, including auto accident claims. For now, though, we will go on to other ways to reduce auto insurance costs.

Duplicate payments

The elimination of duplicate benefit payments should be part of any plan to lower the cost of insurance, not just auto insurance. One whose arm is broken in a car accident could have his medical bills paid by his health insurance, his own auto insurance, and by the other driver's insurance if the court decides it was his fault. In addition, he may be able to collect from his disability insurance for time lost at his job and collect his lost wages a second time from the other driver's insurance company when the lawsuit is settled. If he was driving for his employer at the time, he may also collect both his medical bills and his lost wages from his employer's workers' compensation insurance coverage. He could also collect from his own health and disability insurance policies and from the uninsured motorist portion of his auto insurance policy, if the other driver was uninsured.

Examples of this sort of duplication abound, some of which can be recovered by insurance companies in managing claims. Pursuit of the recovery of duplicate payments, however, is frequently too expensive, and the excess payments go either undetected or ignored. Regardless of which insurance policies are involved, the total insurance system is paying the same bills too many times. This systemwide duplication is reflected in many types of insurance premiums—auto, health, disability, life, uninsured motorists, workers' compensation, and liability insurance. The problem with high-cost insurance is not limited to auto, and the problem of duplicate payments contributes to all of them: insurance customers pay the bills.

In the 1990 Gallup poll mentioned in Chapter 5, 85 percent of survey respondents opposed such duplicate payments. This list recommends ways to eliminate duplication in payments:

- Enact laws to prohibit "stacking" or multiplying insurance benefit payments under different policies applicable to the same injuries—no-fault policies, liability policies, uninsured motorist coverages, medical insurance, and disability insurance, among others.

- Provide options whereby insureds can choose discounts on their insurance premiums by selecting to apply their own benefit policies to auto-related injuries or use deductibles to eliminate duplication of payments.

- Repeal collateral source rules of evidence in lawsuits so all sources of compensation to accident victims are known when damage awards are determined.

- Require disclosure of pertinent information regarding payments made for medical expenses where claims for payments are being made.

- Provide incentives for insurance buyers and claimants to coordinate payments of benefits among applicable policies.

It is not at present illegal for injured people to collect twice for their medical expenses and lost wages. In many cases, such as when the collateral source rule is applied, they are *encouraged* to conceal other benefits and payments to get more from the other party's insurance company. The legal fraternity defends this expensive practice, but it should be stopped. The purpose of insurance is to make people whole again, not to enrich them unduly.

Duplicate payments will decrease when one of two things happen: either the insurance system provides incentives and rewards for people who choose to coordinate their benefits and do not collect twice, or duplicate payments can no longer be legally concealed.

Auto repair costs

The amount paid by auto insurers to repair cars rose at double the rate of inflation between 1981 and 1988, according to a study by the National Association of Insurance Commissioners. More than half the cost of repairing a damaged car goes to buy the replacement parts. Cosmetic parts, such as fenders, door skins, bumpers, grilles, and hoods, have been the subject of a contentious debate about the safety of replacement parts manufactured by the original maker of the car as opposed to those made by competing companies. The parts made by companies other than the original manufacturer generally cost between 25 and 40 percent less than those made by the original equipment manufacturer (OEM). The Insurance Institute for Highway Safety conducted tests of hoods to determine whether OEM versus non-OEM competing parts had any relevance in the safety debate. All parts tested in the crash tests demonstrated that there was no difference among competing replacement hoods. All met federal safety standards that require them to crumple properly so that they do not thrust through to front-seat passengers. For many replacement parts, the argument has been over the quality of sheet metal. Competitive non-OEM sheet metal parts, however, continue to prove of quality equal to OEM parts. Auto manufacturers have no evidence to support their "not safe" argument in their efforts to prevent use of competing parts.

Original manufacturers have resisted competition from other parts makers because the profit margins in replacement parts are high. Before the 1970s there was no alternative to original manufacturer parts. While competition from other parts makers has forced the original manufacturers to bring down their prices somewhat, the cost to replace a car part by part is still triple the original price of the car, and suppliers have proved they will work hard to hang on to this system. In fact, manufacturers have successfully lobbied in several states for laws that restrict the sale of non-OEM parts. Usually these laws appear as disclosure requirements that provide consumers with information about what parts will be used in the repair of their cars. The problem is that these statements wrongly imply that competitive parts are inferior to those of the original equipment manufacturer. The consumer is thus encouraged to insist on original parts, driving up the cost of repairs.

Insurers are obligated by the language of the auto insurance policy to provide insureds with replacement parts equal to or comparable with the originals. When competitive parts of equal or better quality are available for a lower price, insurers recommend use of those parts to keep costs down. Some insureds still want parts from the original manufacturer used in their repairs. In fact, however, many non-OEM parts made by competitors are comparable in quality to those made by the original manufacturer of the car. Many even advertise that they guarantee their parts for as long as the owner keeps the car: even the original manufacturers do not make that promise.

Anticompetitive laws create unwarranted monopolies for original-parts manufacturers, costing consumers and insurance customers unnecessary additional expense. Of course, competitive parts manufacturers should be held to rigid standards for safety and performance to protect consumers. There are some cheap competitive parts on the market that are *not* comparable in quality and safety, and consumers should be protected from receiving these unknowingly. Nevertheless, competition among manufacturers should be encouraged through regulations that provide consumers with guarantees for quality work and quality parts that are certified equal to or better than the original maker's parts. States should resist pressure to enact laws that give original manufacturers any competitive advantage.

The second area where auto repair costs have been escalating dramatically is windshield replacement. According to Safeco Insurance Company, the average windshield has increased from $350 to over $1,000 in only a few years, driving up costs for comprehensive coverage. Most of the increase has been attributable to technological innovations in windshield design, such as shatter-resistant treatments, sun screens, rain-sensitive layers, glass heaters, and even electronic displays. It is estimated, however, that up to 15 percent of all damaged windshields could be repaired instead of replaced, at a cost of less than $100 per windshield. Safeco is encouraging its customers to consider windshield repair when appropriate, and rewarding customers who opt for repair by waiving the comprehensive deductible. Safeco's windshield cost-containment program includes a special arrangement with auto-glass repair companies to ensure quality work and safe repairs for its customers.

The third area of concern is competition among repair shops. To illustrate what can be done here, we will cite two examples: one program established by the California State Automobile Association (CSAA), which writes auto insurance for over 1 million cars in northern California, and the other by Allstate Insurance Company, one of the largest writers of auto insurance in the nation.

CSAA established its Approved Auto Repair program to ensure quality repairs through shops that guarantee their work. Customers receive a list of repair facilities where honest, competent repairs will be done. Claimants are not required to use a repair shop from the CSAA list, but the insurer gives it to them as a service. CSAA monitors the repair shops in its program to gauge customer satisfaction, garage performance, and quality of work. CSAA guarantees any work done at its direction at any shop participating in the Approved Auto Repair program.

Another program, Allstate Insurance Company's Priority Repair Option, was also designed to guarantee quality repairs and superior service for its customers. In practice, it provides a customer base for shops participating in its direct repair program and also a more efficient means for estimating repairs and securing payment for the repair shop. This simple settlement process allows the participating facilities to reduce their marketing and administrative expenses, thus reducing the cost of repairs.

Allstate, however, has taken the program one step farther, working hard with the repair shops to control costs, particularly costs for labor and parts. Allstate conducts inspections of portions of work done by the shops to check quality, customer satisfaction, and costs. This method of control is less expensive for Allstate than having every damaged auto inspected by a claims adjuster. The only hindrance to further success for Allstate's program is that some states prohibit the company from providing a list of recommended repair shops unless the customer specifically asks for a referral. This restriction reduces claimant utilization of the Priority Repair Option and eliminates the opportunity for some of the savings possible through the company's cost-control efforts.

The CSAA and Allstate programs illustrate ways to promote quality repairs at competitive prices and service to the insured by both the insurer and the repair shop. Not all states allow insurance companies to refer claimants to particular repair and body shops, thus protecting the consumer's ability to select any shop he wanted to use and avoiding "restraints" on trade. These programs, however, clearly demonstrate that consumer choice can be preserved while costs are controlled. Insurers should not be allowed to force consumers to use a particular repair facility. But barriers to the efficient handling of claims for auto repairs should be removed.

Stopping claims crime

Finally, we turn to the subject of insurance claims crime, a profitable and largely unpunished illegal business. The Insurance Crime Prevention Institute, National Auto Theft Bureau, Insurance Committee for Arson Control, and Special Investigative Units—all funded by the insurance companies and ultimately by the insurance customers—are pursuing ways to handle this problem. Their contributions to insurance crime detection, investigation, and prosecution are extremely important. Cooperative programs with the FBI, district attorneys, the Justice Department, state highway patrols, local law enforcement, and others involved in putting criminals out of business are essential to stopping insurance claims crime.

In the largest such fraud bust in U.S. history, law-enforcement officers recently rounded up fifty-one insurance-fraud suspects in southern California accused of filing phony accident claims estimated to have cost policyholders over $45 million. Among them were two doctors and a former lawyer who were charged with preparing false medical reports and injury claims that were submitted to insurance companies for payment. The Los Angeles district attorney said, "This whole problem of auto insurance fraud can scarcely be exaggerated. These are people who are involved in very sophisticated schemes that go on and on for extended periods of time." The arrests in this case came after undercover officers infiltrated two large fraud rings. These rings were able to collect on hundreds of false claims because they were submitted for relatively small amounts, usually less than $50,000, and were settled quickly by insurance companies to avoid costly and time-consuming litigation, according to the district attorney.

The claims schemes are generally of three types. In one, a suspect pulls his car in front of another car and then slams on the brakes, causing the unsuspecting motorist to hit him from behind. The suspect then claims injuries and damages against the victim's insurance. In the second, suspects use two vehicles, one insured and one not. The uninsured car is loaded with three or four people. They stage an accident, and later the passengers complain of injuries and file claims. The third type of scheme involves highly sophisticated "paper accidents" in which no cars are actually crashed. Those who submit the claims are provided a script of the incident. Medical claims forms are created by colluding doctors and lawyers.

Los Angeles and other cities hard hit by claims crime have formed special task forces to deal with the problem. Los

Angeles's success with its program has forced fraud rings to move on to Orange County and northern California. Those areas must now gear up to deal with the new wave of auto-accident criminals. It is a national problem, and it will be solved only by concentrated and coordinated efforts of law-enforcement authorities and insurers.

Insurance claims crime is so lucrative that it continues to attract large numbers of participants. Too often, though, when insurance criminals are caught they are not prosecuted with the same severity as other serious criminals. Punishment is often a fine and a slap on the wrist.

All insurance claims crime is theft—theft of insurance customers' funds. Those who want to pay less for insurance, especially for fraudulent claims, must join the battle against claims crime. We can no longer afford to look the other way when we suspect someone is cheating on an insurance claim or when we see evidence of phony claims. We can no longer rationalize inaction by believing that it is just money from an insurance company: it is our money.

Clearly, only a concerted effort of law-enforcement officials, insurance companies, crime detection organizations, lawmakers, the courts, and insurance buyers will curb the cost of insurance crime. These general steps must be part of our insurance crime-cutting program:

- Enact laws that describe insurance fraud and theft as crimes; increase the serious nature of the crime as defined in the law.

- Increase mandatory penalties—both fines and jail terms—for serious and intentional insurance crimes.

- Prohibit courts from giving only perfunctory punishment to repeat offenders.

- Require restitution from all insurance criminals—making them pay back the cost of what they have stolen or what was lost to the defrauding scheme.

- Establish permanent partnerships of insurance companies and law enforcement to detect, investigate, and prosecute insurance crimes.

- Establish training programs for insurance company claims handlers and law enforcement to improve their ability to detect crimes.

- Promote public awareness and support of insurance crime prevention and prosecution programs.

Insurance crime is no different than any other type of crime, except that people generally are not outraged when they see it or hear about it. We should be outraged, however, since it is our money that is being stolen.

Information Strategies

Improving insurance company operations and consumer information services should be part of any plan to reform the insurance system. In Chapter 2 we noted that insurance company operations and overhead, not including taxes, represented on average $19 out of every $100 in auto insurance revenue. We also saw that in comparison with other service businesses this proportion is not out of line. Individual insurance companies, though, range well above and well below this average. Differences among company expenses are primarily the result of different marketing systems and different types of insurance offered.

More than 3,000 insurance companies write property and casualty insurance in this country. The business is competitive by all measures of competition applied by economists and other analysts. Despite the loud pronouncements of industry critics, the industry is not monolithic or anticompetitive. No one insurance company writes more than 10 percent of the property and casualty business in the nation. No one company is able to control the insurance market. Even in the auto insurance business, the largest insurer of private passenger autos in the country insures only 18 percent of all cars. Some companies write only commercial insurance and provide engineering, loss control, and risk-management services to commercial customers. Depending on the type of service provided and the type of insurance written, company overhead as a percentage of premium can vary greatly. The highly varied nature of the insurance needs of businesses and individuals is appropriately met by different service systems.

Competition is the consumer's best guarantee that companies will operate as cost efficiently as possible. Any company that has higher expenses will have to justify the extra cost to its customers or lose business. Some higher-cost insurers do justify their price by providing special services, safety programs, dividend arrangements, or other features. And consumers with a need for those services can decide if that is the best way for them to obtain both the insurance and the service. Company management must find the right balance between the need to serve customers and the mandate to control overhead. Good service requires well-trained and experienced people who can provide the assistance the customer needs.

While everyone will agree that premiums must be high enough to cover the cost of claims and overhead, premiums must also be low enough to attract and retain customers. Insurance companies have built-in incentives to control the cost of claims and to maintain an efficient internal operation, controlling overhead costs. In the current climate of customer dissatisfaction over the high cost of auto insurance, companies have an obligation to be thorough in their efforts to cut any waste in their operations while improving their service to consumers.

The single best way for insurance companies to improve their service is to give their customers more information. The ability to make choices about what we buy, what services we are willing to pay for, and where we will get them is the underlying right of consumer choice. The right to make informed choices about our lives, about how we spend our time and money, is freedom. Consumer choice is empowered by information, but individuals cannot govern their own lives without the information they need to make valid and useful choices.

When people say the price of auto insurance is out of control, they are really saying that they are unable to make choices that will allow them to control their purchase of auto insurance. They cannot, for example, choose not to pay ten cents out of every premium dollar to lawyers and the legal system or to lower their own cost of insurance through elective coordination of their various insurance policies. Told to "shop around" for the best price, they have no means to evaluate what services they will get for different premiums or what the financial standing of the different sellers may be. They are not given information that allows them to buy a new car based upon its crashworthiness and repairability or on the insurance discounts applicable to safety features they desire.

Insurance consumers must be empowered with information that allows them to compare service, products, prices, discounts, and other features offered by different companies. Many state insurance departments publish surveys of consumer complaint ratios, allowing consumers to know which companies had the best and worst records. With that information, a person shopping for auto insurance can cross-check the lowest price against the complaint ratio list and judge for himself whether the low price might lead to service problems. Consumers must also have coverage comparisons, checklists, and buyer's guides. They must also have information about what to do in the event of a loss, where to go with a complaint, and what their rights are in the event of cancellation, nonrenewal, or disputes over premium misquotations. This should be essential information, always available to consumers.

Consumers, though, need still more information. If, for example, a person knew that the car he was about to purchase had the highest theft rate of any make, it would provide another basis for deciding whether to buy the car. If he did decide to buy it, that same information could convince him to install an antitheft device, which would earn him a discount on his comprehensive insurance coverage. The information about theft rates, crashworthiness, repairability, and applicable discounts is precisely the kind that allows consumers to make decisions taking into account the impact on insurance costs of other choices they are making. Consumer insurance decisions should be more than simply deciding how much liability insurance to buy or what coverages to add to the standard homeowners' policy.

The car salesman would probably not like it, but new car window stickers should carry safety, damageability, repairability, and theft-rate information at point of sale, like any other product-labeling program. We believe it is our right to know what is contained in any package or can of food. We also have a right to know the insurance impact of a particular consumer product, especially autos where the costs are significant.

In the political battle over auto insurance reform, consumer knowledge is also important. Public opinion and political pressure is what makes politicians take notice, but so far this power has been missing in the battle for auto insurance reform. When insurance buyers are finally given all the facts about what is causing the rise in auto insurance rates, they will be able to fight the underlying illnesses of the system, instead of the symptoms. Consumer information is the key.

SEVEN

From Blame to Responsibility

I f we want to reform auto insurance, we must move from a system of blame to one of responsibility. This chapter examines the roles and responsibilities of those in a position to change the auto insurance system—insurance companies, their agents, and their customers. We will also look at the role that can be played by government insurance regulators and by legislators. Each of these groups must take responsibility for making the auto insurance system fair and equitable to insurance buyers, claimants, and insurance companies.

Changes in auto insurance will come in two forms, systemic change and individual change. Systemic changes would reform the entire auto insurance system's underlying method of operation, while individual changes are those that consumers, claimants, and those in the insurance business would make. Both kinds of change are necessary if insurance customers are to see meaningful reduction in the price they pay for auto insurance.

Insurers' Responsibilities

As we know, insurers have good business reasons for making the auto insurance system more efficient by controlling claims costs and overhead expenses. Insurance buyers, however, also expect their insurance company to pursue systemic reforms aggressively outside their own business operations. Here is a summary of the basic obligations insurers have to themselves, their agents, and their customers:

- Manage an efficient business operation

- Provide good service when customers are buying insurance—offering information about coverages, rates, and counseling for individual needs; assist each customer in analyzing and managing his own risk through insurance-buying decisions

- Provide good claims service when accidents occur

- Pay claims quickly when they are clearly legitimate and responsibility for payment is known

- Vigorously fight fraudulent or illegitimate claims

- Defend the insureds in any lawsuit brought against them to the full extent of the liability portion of the policy

- Establish fair, cost-based rates for all sections of the auto insurance policy

- Charge enough premium to cover the losses and expenses for the insurance coverage provided

- Remain competitive with other providers in the marketplace

- Ensure that agents and service representatives of the company have adequate training, product, service, and information to meet consumers' needs

- Establish cooperative programs with local law enforcement to crack down on insurance claims fraud and vehicle theft

- Continue support of organizations that conduct research to reduce costs and fight fraud (National Auto Theft Bureau, Insurance Crime Prevention Institute, Insurance Institute for Highway Safety, and others)

- Set up a special division within the company to detect, investigate, and pursue prosecution of fraud crimes—a "special investigative unit"

- Fight to change the auto insurance system in the state legislatures

- Promote safety in vehicle design and manufacture

- Promote safety in road and highway design

- Support strong enforcement of highway traffic control and driving laws; support all efforts to stop drunk and drugged driving

- Establish programs that manage the cost of repairing damaged vehicles, through approved repair programs, aggressive cost controls, and quality guarantees for consumers

Most insurance companies engage in many of these activities. Each company should fully commit itself to these fundamental responsibilities. In addition, the insurer can take the initiative in some other areas for creating a stronger partnership with customers in the all-out attack on costs. Through improved communication and innovation, insurers should concentrate on rebuilding the trust among the company, its agents, and its customers. An insurer can reach out to its own customers by:

- recognizing that customers as a group have great concern about the price of auto insurance and a strong desire to lower costs

- communicating with all customers in clear language about where their insurance premium dollars go, what the money pays for, and who gets it; about the financial status of the company, including profits and costs of doing business; about the value of insurance; about what the company is doing to control costs; about what the consumer can do to help control costs; and about the impact of public policy decisions—how much of their premium pays to subsidize assigned risk, how much goes to pay state premium taxes, how much goes to the guarantee fund, and the like

- lobbying aggressively in state legislatures for the needs of low-income drivers, creating programs that address the affordability problem of qualified low-income citizens

- conducting research to find out what information consumers need about insurance issues, not just for marketing purposes, but about the industry in general—its practices, the laws governing it, the politics of reform, and consumer rights in that process; surveying customers' attitudes and opinions about the insurer's service, products, and related issues

- providing other information about insurance issues, including pro and con views, in regular publications for customers

- promoting the partnership of insurance companies and insurance buyers in the fight against insurance claims fraud, vehicle theft, and other insurance cost problems

- providing premium bills that clearly note discounts for good driving, use of safety or antitheft devices, deductibles, and other cost-saving features

- giving customers incentives and options for cutting their own insurance costs—discounts for coordination of benefits, rewards for cost-cutting behavior and for safety measures, and recognition for claim-free records

- conducting creative two-way communication with customers and agents—establishing decentralized operations that enable the "community" of customers to act in its own interest, conducting "town hall" sessions with agents and insureds locally and regionally, establishing programs that reconnect insureds with the people working in the company and with their agents

- redirecting corporate giving programs to the grass-roots level, based on needs of customers in their communities where employees and agents are already involved

- innovating new insurance products, such as policies with features that eliminate incentives for cost build-up

This last item is particularly important, since the sale of insurance products has usually focused first on benefits, and second on price. In life insurance, for example, the exhortation to sales people was always, "Sell benefits." The emphasis on comparisons of benefits leads to a broadening of coverage, allowing sales representatives to capture a client by offering a policy that covers more than another company's policy. As a result, people sometimes buy more coverage than they really need. Many people have policies whose benefits overlap, covering them for the same medical treatments or other losses. The insurance industry has provided, sometimes by court decision, broader and broader policy forms.

A new approach may entail reversing this trend by allowing consumers to narrow or limit what they buy to save money. A consumer, for example, might choose to limit the types of nonmedical treatments allowed under an insurance policy, excluding things like acupuncture, physiotherapy, or treatment by chiropractors, when not prescribed by a physician. In return for taking that option, the insured would receive a discount. Of course, this approach requires more careful communication with customers but may assist in trimming the customer's insurance costs. Innovation in insurance marketing may require development and promotion of more limited, rather than broader, coverage. If consumers realize that they can save money by forgoing some coverages, this concept could become a way to satisfy consumer demand for lower prices.

An insurance company executive recently told about his company's idea for a lower-cost auto insurance policy. In close analysis of the claim files, the company found a lag time between the occurrence of the auto accident and the company's notification of a claim ranging generally from a few hours to a few weeks. The company discovered that the earlier it receives the notice, the better service it can provide, the better able it is to learn the facts of the accident, and the better able it is to settle quickly and fairly. When the company is not informed about an accident or claim for several weeks, the ultimate costs are much higher—both the cost of the claim and the cost to settle.

The company's objective is to cut the cost of claims by encouraging customers to report claims immediately. To do that, it has established a twenty-four-hour a day, seven-day-a-week, toll-free claims hotline. The company has made claims reporting convenient and is considering going one step further: a discounted policy that obligates the customer to report any accident within twenty-four hours. If a customer failed to report within the twenty-four-hour period, the company would cover the claim in the usual way but would not offer the discount option to the customer at renewal or would make some other adjustment. Although the concept is not fully developed, it is encouraging that someone is thinking about a way to offer lower-cost insurance. If the company is confident that early claims reporting will save money and will pass those savings along to consumers, then the competitive insurance market is functioning as it should.

That simple innovation would offer individual customers a chance to save on their insurance in exchange for an adjustment in their own behavior. While this kind of product innovation is needed in the insurance business, unfortunately, the trend toward greater regulation of rates and policy forms diminishes innovation rather than encouraging it.

While insurers have tried to do many of the things on the preceding list, one thing seems to be missing in their efforts. Insurance companies approach problems from an economic point of view, trying to find and explain the economic solutions as they see them. What they have failed to take into account is the human emotions of their customers, who struggle to pay the premiums and are angry about the high cost. It is not enough for insurance companies simply to point out the economic problems underlying the auto insurance crisis and to plead with customers to understand that they did not cause these escalating costs. Customers need to be shown that their company is a cost-cutting champion. Companies must give customers the information that will motivate them to push for change in the insurance system. Customers must know what is causing their premiums to rise, information that allows them to judge what is right and wrong about where the money goes. When customers have options for controlling their own risks and costs and when they know their efforts to reduce costs will pay off in lower prices, then the partnership of insurance companies and insurance buyers will begin to work.

Rebuilding trust with customers must be the insurer's highest priority, and it can be achieved only through better communication—excellence in information service to customers. Then insurance buyers and their insurance companies together can repair the auto insurance system.

Individuals' Responsibilities

The individual insurance customer makes fairly simple demands on the insurance system. He wants the ability to control the risks related to his ownership and use of an automobile—the freedom and security the insurance premium buys. The policyholder also wants to be able to control the cost of that freedom and security. That individual is a member of a community of insurance customers, and therefore must take responsibility for his place in that community:

- Drivers must drive responsibly. This seems obvious but is important. Drivers have a responsibility to keep their cars in safe running order, know and abide by traffic laws, drive sober, and respect the lives and property of others on the road. In fact, the community that relies on the individual driver to do this is much larger than the insurance customers' community: every person's life, health, family, and property are endangered by the poor or reckless driving habits of others. Cars are inherently dangerous, and it is up to each driver to control his own car.

- Each driver must pay his fair share into the system. Each insurance customer has the obligation to pay the premium appropriate for his level of risk. He must be completely honest on the insurance application, giving accurate and complete information to the agent, so the policy will be rated and quoted fairly. To do otherwise cheats the community of insurance customers. As insurance buyers, we must see ourselves as part of that community, with a responsibility to the other members.

- When an accident does occur, each claimant should expect to receive a fair settlement for his losses, not a ticket to the lawsuit lottery or an opportunity to collect duplicate payments for the same damage. The claimant should notify the insurance company of the accident immediately and should look for a settlement that makes him "whole" again economically. Anything more comes at the expense of the community of insurance buyers, including the claimant.

- Insurance buyers can promote their own self-interest by being intolerant of insurance fraud, claims cheating, and other practices that drive up costs of the claims settlement system.

- Individuals can take precautions against losses by installing antitheft devices on cars, buying cars with the latest safety technology, wearing seatbelts and requiring their passengers to do likewise.

- Insurance buyers should take responsibility for being knowledgeable consumers—demanding information about discounts for coordination of benefits, antitheft and safety devices, deductibles, and other premium-saving options.

- During the claims settlement process, individuals should give the claims system a chance before they file a lawsuit. They can ask the insurance adjuster about qualified and competitive repair shops and other cost-saving programs.

- Individuals should support the efforts of insurance companies and law enforcement to attack the problems of drunk driving, auto theft, and claims fraud by keeping a watchful eye for suspicious accidents, reporting criminal acts, and being willing to testify.

- Insurance consumers must be tough customers—shopping around for the best coverages, most competitive prices, and best services and using the consumer information services of the state insurance department.

In the final analysis, insurance consumers are the key to changing the political stalemate that has allowed the system to become what it is. In the insurance system, they pay premiums; in the political arena, they vote. They must convert their anger over high auto insurance costs to pressure for legislative action. Armed with information about what hurts their interests, they can override the usual political muddling and deal-making that lead to "no-real-change" legislation.

Regulators' Responsibilities

The most important responsibilities of insurance regulators are to oversee the financial condition of insurance companies and to promote competition. When an insurance company goes broke, its policyholders and claimants are the losers. The job of the state insurance department is to ensure that insurance consumers and injured people will not lose because of financial weakness of an insurance company. Consumers must be able to trust that their insurer will be there to respond with payment and defense when they are in an accident. Insurance regulators in every state are the first line of protection consumers have from this fear.

Insurance laws, regulations, and statutes vary from state to state. Likewise, the role of the insurance regulator—whether called a division of insurance, department of insurance, insurance commission, or other name—also varies. Common to all state insurance regulators, though, is the responsibility to scrutinize company finances, anticipate which companies will have trouble, take steps to correct their problems, and ultimately deal with the failed companies. Regulators guard the pool of insurance customers' funds from being lost through sloppy operations or fraudulent practices.

Financial troubles of an insurance company can arise for any number of reasons. Some result from too-rapid growth, when a company takes on more risk than its financial standing will bear and the losses overrun its revenue. Similarly, a company may write business that is riskier than at first thought, resulting in premiums inadequate to pay the losses. Financial problems can also occur when courts interpret insurance policies to cover losses unintended when the policy was written, expanding the coverage and damage awards by court verdict. If the original premium is too low for the ultimate liability insured, the company will run into financial difficulties. Others experience problems when regulators do not allow the companies to raise rates and the premiums collected begin to lag behind losses. In the worst cases, companies fail to set aside enough money to pay future claims, cover up their deteriorating financial condition, and then suddenly collapse.

The regulator conducts examinations of company books and records, not just those submitted to the regulator's office but those in the offices of the companies. The regulator looks for signs of financial trouble, like mounting losses, excessive premium growth without proper underwriting control, risky investment practices, writing business outside the company's area of expertise, poor management of operations, and imprudent or dishonest activities. This oversight requires an army of well-trained field examiners, auditors, and actuaries who are empowered to force companies to comply with specific laws and regulations, to cease various activities, to establish certain practices, and to pay fines and other penalties. Ultimately, the regulator can suspend or revoke an insurer's license to do business in the state.

Most industry observers and insurance regulators agree that the majority of insurance companies are financially sound. The number of insolvencies and the amount required to make good on the claims against failed companies, however, have risen in recent years. The role of the regulator is therefore as critical for insurance companies as for savings and loans and banks: the job is the same, protecting consumers' funds. The best way to accomplish that is to prevent insolvencies through corrective and disciplinary action; mopping up after a company goes under is much worse.

When companies do go bankrupt, the regulator must take care of the claims people would have expected the now-insolvent company to pay. Most states have a "guarantee" fund to satisfy these claims. After the regulator liquidates the failed company, salvaging whatever remains, he turns the rest over to the guarantee fund manager who handles the claims until all are settled. Money for the guarantee fund is created through an assessment on all other insurance companies writing the same type of business in the state, an assessment then passed on directly to policyholders. The guarantee fund system is an important means of taking care of injured people and others who have claims so that they will not be abandoned because of the failure of an insurance company. The insurance buyers, though, are the ones who eventually share in the cost of those claims.

In the view of the insurance buyers, the regulator's role becomes even more important. Not only is the regulator expected to protect the pool of funds, but is also expected to guard against possible future failures of other insurers to avoid the insolvency bailouts.

Poorly run companies will fail, whether they are savings and loans, insurance companies, or grocery stores. The business of insurance is regulated because those failures can harm the large population of insurance buyers and claimants. Because overseeing the financial condition of insurance companies is the single most important function of regulators, state insurance departments must be adequately funded and staffed to accomplish this job. That funding must be provided by legislatures through state budgets and should not be compromised.

Insurance departments regulate a lot more than insurer financial operations, of course. Regulators should also work to promote competition. But in recent years we have seen a trend toward greater regulation, which is actually misapplied. Regulators have attempted to control insurance prices rather than dealing with the causes behind price increases. Again, they are trying to control the symptoms of disease without attacking the illness itself.

Regulation of rates by insurance departments ranges from very strict to very loose. At the strictest end of the scale, "prior approval" requires that all insurance rates be approved in advance. At the other end of the scale, "open competition" allows insurance companies to set their own prices and the marketplace controls rates through competition among companies.

California's Proposition 103 changed that state from an open competition state to a prior approval state. What those who drafted the new law failed to do, though, was to treat any of the underlying sicknesses of the auto insurance system. Proposition 103 attacked the symptoms of an inefficient system by ordering companies to lower rates and forcing them to get approval in advance for rate hikes. Nothing in Proposition 103 cuts legal overhead, eliminates fraud or abuse, or stops cars from being stolen. In fact, the huge regulatory apparatus set up by Proposition 103 will cost insurance consumers millions of dollars in expense without delivering one dollar of savings.

Study after study has compared strict prior approval states with open competition states. So far, no difference has been found to justify all the extra regulatory overhead used to regulate insurer rates. Competition, in most cases, is more effective in keeping consumer prices low. The fact is, however, that people believe they are paying too much for insurance and see rate regulation as a solution. We will therefore have a lot of it in the next few years.

But regulation will never solve the underlying problems of auto claims expenses, the perverse incentives that drive costs up. Real change in the $77 that goes to the cost of claims out of every $100 in insurance revenue will require reforms that have very little to do with the system applied by regulators to determine rates.

Rate regulation is essential, however, to ensure that rates are fair for all types of consumers, that rating schemes are not unfairly discriminatory, and that rating and underwriting practices of insurers are reasonable. If a state adopts a flexible rate regulation system, the insurance regulator will be able to promote fair competition that benefits consumers, while still overseeing discipline in the marketplace.

In addition to regulating insurer rates in the marketplace, regulators must also regulate the forms and language used in insurance policies sold to consumers. This is a difficult responsibility since slight differences in policy language can mean large differences in coverage for consumers. If all auto policies are identical, then each insurance buyer will have the same coverage in the event of loss. While this close similarity may make it easy to shop for the best price, it does not provide the flexibility to meet consumers' needs and desires for different coverage, policy features, or discount options. A consumer shopping for lettuce in the market will find five different varieties at five different prices. At least there the buyer can see each type and price and make a choice based on taste and budget. If an insurance policy is offered with five different deductible options or discount features for different sections of the contract, the consumer may have trouble determining what is best for his needs. It is just these options, however, that allow consumers, with assistance from their agents, to tailor the insurance to individual need and budget.

The insurance regulator has an important role in determining that the policy provisions and forms will be unambiguous and fair. The regulator must encourage competition through product innovation, while ensuring that consumers will not be disadvantaged by some unusual policy language. The regulator must protect consumers from unfair policy forms but must not constrain the marketplace from offering a variety of insurance products and options.

Beyond its responsibilities for monitoring insurer solvency and rate and form regulation, each insurance department must be a force for fairness in claims settlement and claims-handling practices. The department must provide consumers with a mechanism for filing complaints about claims or any other problem they are having with their insurance. The insurance department should also establish a fraud unit with specific responsibility for working on those problems with companies, law enforcement, and individual consumers.

Finally, the insurance regulators must supply information to policy makers, legislators, consumers, and the press. In their own state, they are a primary source of insurance data, statistics, surveys, and analyses of all kinds. The information provided by the insurance department can help form the basis for development of new laws and regulations. The information emerging from these departments should focus the public policy debate on the underlying issues to provide lawmakers a factual base for decisions in the best interests of consumers. These studies can show, for example, if consumer needs for insurance are being met or if certain types of insurance are readily available in all areas of the state. The regulator can tabulate complaints filed by consumers to determine complaint records for companies and then provide that information to consumers so they can compare company services and prices. Regulators can also survey company services, compile rating comparisons and other information for distribution to the public, and make buyers' guides available for all types of insurance.

The insurance regulator is the arm of government responsible for protecting consumers who use insurance to manage their risks. Safeguarding the financial soundness of insurance companies should be the highest priority among the many tasks of the regulator. Empowering insurance buyers to be effective consumers in the marketplace, though, is clearly their next-highest priority.

Legislators' Responsibilities

Politicians make easy targets for having allowed the auto insurance mess to degenerate, especially in the states where legislative efforts have stalemated or consumers have had to choose among complex proposals at the ballot box. There are no simple answers, no single solution, and no easy reforms that will restore the auto insurance situation. While political rhetoric and campaign slogans may continue to promise simple solutions and lower rates, those promises rarely include straightforward information about the necessary trade-offs, that is, what it will take to make real change in the way the auto accident claims system is run. The political system rarely requires such candor, since the usual method of doing business in the state capitols is to negotiate a compromise among the interested parties. This system rarely offends or hurts any one group, but rarely satisfies anyone either. And often powerful interests are "more equal" than consumers. With complex problems like auto insurance, political solutions have not worked: they usually complicate things further, making real solutions harder to attain. If legislators voted for what was really in the best interest of the majority, here is what would be instituted:

- a set of laws to govern the business of insurance, promoting fair competition, ensuring the financial integrity of insurance companies, and overseeing fair practices in insurance sales and claims handling

- adequate funding through premium tax revenues for the regulator's important consumer protection role, not just for the insurance regulator but also for efforts to control insurance fraud and auto theft and for consumer safety and education

- healthy competition both in the business of insurance and in the businesses that provide the services purchased with claims payments

- promotion of driver, vehicle, and highway safety—such as mandatory seatbelt laws, motorcycle headgear requirements, laws to prevent or crack down on drunk and drugged driving

- programs that deter insurance claims fraud and prevent vehicle theft and other abuses

- stiff mandatory penalties for insurance claims crimes and for repeat offenders of traffic laws; effective law enforcement in dealing with insurance fraud and claims crime

- elimination of duplicate payments of claims and of concealment of duplicate sources of compensation for losses

- balanced reform measures that do not compromise or weaken the trade-offs essential for cost savings, especially for legal reform; options for consumers to choose between guaranteed benefits insurance for themselves or liability insurance

- removal of the incentives for cost build-up in claims

- approaches that close the gaps in the private insurance system through carefully designed public programs, such as an assigned risk plan for drivers with poor records or joint underwriting authorities for market segments not served by private companies

- legal and economic incentives for low-income drivers to buy insurance through specific programs designed to meet their needs

Low-Income Drivers

While the affordability problem for low-income drivers has been discussed elsewhere in this book, it deserves more attention because of its relationship to the uninsured motorist problem. Even if all the systemic and individual changes discussed in the preceding chapters are implemented, some people will still be unable to afford auto insurance. Low-income drivers, particularly in urban centers where insurance costs more, will still have difficulty paying for insurance. These drivers, many of whom drive in violation of the compulsory insurance laws, are uninsured only because the price of auto insurance is prohibitive at their income: they do not willingly break the law.

In earlier chapters, we have seen that uninsured drivers cause great concern for insured drivers, who are paying more for their own insurance because of uninsured vehicles on the roads. This concern translates into political pressure to solve the problem of uninsured motorists. Politicians have responded by making insurance mandatory but have not solved the problem of making it affordable. Drivers who can afford insurance but who refuse to buy it are an enforcement problem, and additional enforcement is the solution. The problem of drivers who cannot afford insurance and thus do not buy it, however, cannot be addressed with an enforcement solution.

Society has solved problems for low-income people in other areas through government programs designed to make certain essential products and services more affordable and available. Food stamps provide food for those who qualify, Medicaid covers a portion of health-care costs for low-income people, and various housing programs subsidize shelter for qualified families. In a compassionate society, especially one as affluent as the United States, the needs of the poor are looked after by the public. Although we may be concerned about the structure, efficiency, or growing abuse of some of these programs, most do not argue about the need for them.

If auto insurance is required by law for all drivers and people expect that it will be affordable since its purchase is mandatory, then government has a role in making it possible for low-income drivers to carry it, especially the working poor who need their cars to keep their jobs. The failure of our political system to solve the affordability problem for low-income drivers has heightened the auto insurance crisis—not just for the low-income uninsured driver but for all other drivers, for insurance companies, and especially for politicians.

There is a solution. It lies in examining other programs for qualified low-income people, in recognizing their special need within the auto insurance system, and in crafting a government policy to meet that need. Any such effort must be a cooperative venture of private insurance and government that respects the individual drivers whose income forces them to seek assistance in securing insurance. The program would require some subsidy, just as food stamps and Medicaid do, but must also require the participating drivers to share the burden and responsibility for buying the insurance coverage. In addition, it must also provide these drivers with an incentive for maintaining a good driving record and allow them to become part of the community of insured drivers rather than excluding them from the system.

Other programs for low-income people show clearly that some formula for subsidization is the fairest method of meeting their needs. For auto insurance, a successful program for low-income drivers would incorporate many of these recommendations:

- Private insurance companies would handle both distribution and service of the insurance policies and the claims arising from the policies.

- Insurance companies conducting private auto insurance business in a state would be required to offer the policy and could not refuse to issue a policy to a qualified low-income driver.

- Low-income individuals would purchase the insurance through a system of vouchers that would be issued in amounts linked to an individual's or household's income, verified through state tax returns.

- Vouchers would be subsidized through a public financing program determined by legislators but structured to avoid their use as currency, as has occurred with food stamps.

- Qualified recipients of vouchers would purchase insurance from a private insurance company, using the voucher, but would be responsible for paying some premium. Vouchers would not cover the total cost of a basic insurance policy.

- Low-income drivers would be allowed to choose any insurance company based on products, services, and other features. Drivers could choose to buy amounts and types of insurance in addition to the basic policy subsidized by the voucher. Low-income drivers would thus retain their economic choices in the marketplace.

- Low-income drivers with bad driving records would not be subsidized through public funds beyond the voucher amount allowed through the means test. The driver's record would still affect the total premium collected by the insurance company, and drivers with poor records would be responsible for paying the increased cost caused by their driving record.

- Consumers ineligible for receiving vouchers under the income test established by the state would not be subsidized by public funds or by other drivers, as now occurs with many assigned risk programs.

This brief list outlines a solution to the insurance affordability problem faced by low-income drivers, politicians, and insurance companies. Low-income drivers who want to be insured and drive legally would have their needs met by such a program. Politicians, desperate to deal with both the social and the economic issues intertwined in the auto insurance crisis, have a special responsibility to meet the needs of low-income drivers. In addition, insurance companies that recognize their own economic difficulty in aiding low-income drivers have a responsibility to pursue aggressively solutions to the affordability problems of all drivers, not just those who now buy auto insurance. Every other driver on the road concerned about the record numbers of uninsured drivers will appreciate a solution that adds more people to the community of insurance buyers—

leaving them less at risk of being in an accident with an un-insured driver.

Conclusion

The community of insurance customers, along with agents and companies, must pursue ways for the auto insurance system to address real costs and to allow all drivers to be insured. How, then, can we achieve lower costs and reduce the number of uninsured drivers? Doing so will require that legislators swim upstream, so to speak, against their normal methods of operation—brokering among affected parties. The simple but novel suggestion made here is that legislators should pass laws without negotiating away the real reforms needed to repair the auto insurance system. Leg-islators will do this only if their constituents, the driving public, demand it. Unless drivers, insured or not, use their political power to bolster the political will of their legislative representatives to face this very difficult job of no-nonsense auto insurance reform, real changes will not take place. If every driver exercises that po-litical power, real reform is possible.

EIGHT

The Principles

A uto insurance claims are out of control and insurance customers are outraged. They should be. A lot of their money is paying off lawyers, "emotional damage" claims, car thieves, claims criminals, and uninsured drivers. Only 10 percent of the auto insurance dollar goes for provision of medical care to the injured—one of the main reasons auto insurance exists. Control is not now vested in those who pay *into* the system but perversely in those who are paid *by* the system. If the cost of insurance is not brought under control, affordability and availability problems will spread, even to states that now have lower auto insurance costs. And if the affordability problems of low-income drivers are not solved, the political and social pressure surrounding the auto insurance crisis will continue to mount. The way auto insurance dollars are spent on the claims side must align with the priorities of those paying the tab—the community of insurance buyers.

This community of insurance buyers is huge, and does not lend itself easily to effective organization. Social cohesion tends to break down in large-scale enterprises. The sheer size of modern institutions, whether governmental or private, makes it very difficult for individuals to have any sense of control over the direction of their "community." American taxpayers, for instance, know this well: most see their taxes falling into some black hole, paying for all sorts of excesses, with no one protecting their interests. Taxes keep going up, seemingly without accountability to the individual taxpayer.

The economic self-interest of insurance buyers would presumably dictate that their money be used by and large to help injured people and to repair and replace damaged property—and that these be done as efficiently as possible. Helping the injured and repairing property were the original purposes for creating a way to share the economic risks associated with auto accidents, a purpose served only when expenditures for other purposes are cut to the absolute minimum. In addition, company overhead and sales expense must cover only what is clearly necessary to operate the business properly and provide good service to consumers. Payments to lawyers must be cut from the system, except when representation by a lawyer is critical to just treatment of a claimant. We must make an all-out effort to eliminate payments to car thieves and insurance claim criminals and an even greater effort to prevent all kinds of losses, especially those caused by drunk and drugged drivers.

When the premium dollar helps injured people and repairs damaged property, *and not much else,* and when insurance buyers *know* where the money goes, then they will be satisfied that they are getting good value for their premium dollars.

Community action is the most effective tool for social change. The community of insurance buyers, however, is not grounded in traditional forms of community—family, church, local civic group, or neighborhood. Modern, urban society requires a new form of community composed of nontraditional groups brought together by their common economic needs and values—in this case, insurance buyers sharing the risk and the cost of misfortune.

This community has a clear self-interest in controlling and governing how its economic resources are spent. Insurance companies, as trustees of the economic resources of their customers, have a fundamental obligation to be full partners in the efforts of the insurance buyers to be self-governing. As we have shown, insurers have the responsibility of providing customers with information that empowers them to act in their own self-interest, both collectively and individually. This information responsibility is the key to the partnership of insurance sellers and insurance buyers. No other single element will go as far in rebuilding trust between insurers and their customers—and there is a big job to be done.

Because the trust has so badly deteriorated, many insurance customers may not be willing to accept information provided by the insurance industry. In some areas of the country, the anger and frustration of insurance customers has built a huge emotional wall between them and their insurance company. Individual agents and service representatives, who deal day-to-day with insurance customers, are the key to breaking down that wall and regaining customers' confidence.

As we have seen throughout the preceding chapters, many things will have to be done before consumers can find meaningful savings. Moreover, informed consumers must act collectively as a community in partnership with insurance companies and agents to get the job done.

Why would insurance buyers want to be partners with insurance companies and agents in the effort to control the cost of auto insurance? Why not develop partnerships with other groups to pursue lower costs? The question really is, With whom should consumers work to seek lower costs? Who best can represent their interests? Certainly politicians, policy makers, and legislatures would seem likely candidates for such a partnership. As we have seen, however, the need for political compromise has prevented politicians from acting effectively on behalf of insurance buyers, even though these individuals represent a majority of voting constituents. Why? Because voters have not sent a single clear message to legislators—not yet, anyway.

As for other partners, we can probably omit those who primarily take money out of the auto claims system. This group includes doctors, hospitals, auto repair shops, and lawyers, with the latter being an especially interesting study. The lawyers frequently portray themselves in the debate about auto insurance as the defenders of injured people and those at the mercy of insurance companies or "the system." Who is surprised that lawyers' advertising tells consumers not to trust their insurance company? The last thing a lawyer would want is a trusting partnership between insurance companies and their customers. The trial lawyer's self-interest feeds on an environment without trust, where everyone sues. While they may help an injured person in court, their involvement in auto insurance claims harms the overall economic interests of insurance buyers. They do not represent the interests of the large group of insurance buyers but rather only certain claimants. It would be surprising indeed if any proposal offered by trial lawyers for resolving auto insurance problems would trim costs facing insurance buyers without protecting the role of lawyers in the costly business of insurance claims.

Professional consumer advocates have played a very important role in the effort to change the auto insurance system. But some consumer groups have failed to advocate the interests of *all* insurance buyers. Generally, the professional consumer advocate fights for only one segment of the premium-paying public—the rights of accident victims, for example, or the needs of low-income people. A few consumer advocacy groups have close ties to trial lawyers, a relationship that limits their ability to advocate the needs of all insurance consumers objectively. And many consumer advocates spend time attacking the symptoms of higher rates rather than the causes, preferring to concentrate on the process by which rates are approved by the regulator rather than the costs of insurance. There are many different consumer advocates involved in the insurance debate, but thus far they have reached no consensus on solutions to the problem. Their role in voicing the concerns of the community of insurance buyers as a whole, however, is extremely important.

Two allies that insurance consumers should have in this battle are their insurance company and their own insurance agent. The companies are already motivated to keep costs down and to try to find ways to get claims under control for three good reasons: first, it is good for business, which operates under tight competition; second, it will help customers who are unhappy about high costs; and third, it will help reduce the political heat. Insurance companies have an obligation both to their policyholders who trust them with their premiums and to their stockholders who expect them to protect their investment. Both those who invest in insurance companies and those who buy insurance have an interest in lowering the cost of claims. As a result the insurance company must serve both those interests, and thus has a double incentive to assist customers in fighting all the perverse forces that cost them more every year.

The partnership of insurers and customers will benefit both partners over the long run. Insurance agents and customer service representatives are important links in that partnership. Insurance customers need the support of the large insurance companies with their organizations, direct access to information, and ability to communicate. They also need the assistance of individual agents and service people who can help them understand and make informed decisions about their specific needs. Companies benefit, too, from this partnership. They need their customers and agents to develop the groundswell of public pressure to effect political change. That partnership can be enormously powerful in transforming the insurance system; without it, nothing will change.

The auto insurance premium *can* be reduced if insurance buyers as a group decide to mobilize to change the system. Political leaders will not take the initiative to solve the problem, at least not without pressure from large numbers of constituents. But a political mobilization of insurance customers can break the political stalemate, accomplishing everything from lowering the legal overhead and removing the incentives that drive up costs, to tightening up the laws and enforcement on drunk driving and claims crimes.

Suggestions that insurance would be better provided through a state-run system overlook the fact that once any process is bureaucratized, it is no longer accountable to those who use its services. We all know the sad failure of socialized systems around the world: only private communities and private enterprises are forced to respond to customer and community demands. While the purpose of modern welfare programs is to protect individuals from economic misfortune, they lack the discipline and competition of the marketplace. And they can never provide individual autonomy and freedom within a marketplace of competitors.

The insurance mess makes an excellent parallel to current environmental problems. We are all aware of the environmental threats facing this country and the world. Although no one person can change the big picture, if every person takes some responsibility the big picture changes. If every person cuts individual fuel consumption by 10 percent, for instance, we have less pollution and less demand for oil. No one person's 10 percent decrease, by itself, has any impact on air pollution or the global demand for oil, but all consumers together have a huge impact. At the same time, if each person assumes that his contribution is meaningless and does not make the 10 percent effort, then no progress is made on the larger problem.

Recycling programs and other environmental efforts require a common attitude of caring for the future well-being of the larger community. The self-interest of the individual and the future well-being of the community are closely linked. When we see institutions leading the way toward solutions, then each of us is motivated to work individually toward the common goals. Together, we gain confidence in the ability of our institutions, communities, and ourselves to solve problems. Each individual knows that the effort to recycle will work only if everyone does it. In fact, members of the community who work hard toward the common goals have a distinct self-interest in the behavior of other members of the community. Every person in this country who takes the time and trouble to recycle bottles, cans, or newspapers is a member of the community of people concerned about the environment. They do not all have to attend a convention or join a group in order to work collectively and individually to solve a societal problem.

The problems of auto insurance buyers will be fought and won at two levels of community. First, insurance buyers can take individual action. Just as environmental protection depends on a common attitude of caring about the future of the environment, insurance reform success depends on commonly held attitudes that influence how people drive, how they treat the claims process, and how they communicate with their legislators.

Second, insurance buyers can effect change at the community level. A local community plagued by high auto theft, for example, can develop a campaign to discourage it through use of window decals, public education, and installation of individual antitheft devices. Local communities can attack the drunk-driving problem by establishing free-ride programs or stepping up law enforcement. Insurance companies can assist local communities with these efforts. Just as a water company works to help consumers save water during a drought by giving them conservation tips and by monitoring water consumption and rationing programs, insurance companies are uniquely positioned to help communities fight high insurance costs. Companies can identify reasons why one community has higher insurance rates than another and recommend ways to cut costs. With that information, residents can decide how best to deal with the issue locally, what programs to initiate, and how to motivate citizens to become involved.

For insurance companies to control costs effectively, they must rely on the collective concern and individual action of their customers. The rebuilding of trust must be worked in both directions. Insurance companies have learned not to trust claimants and insureds to be honest, while insurance buyers and claimants have come to believe that they will not be treated fairly by insurance companies. Both must think and act differently if the partnership of insurers and customers is to be successful.

The critical player in the effort to rebuild trust between insurance companies and their customers is the insurance agent or customer representative. We can enter into a partnership with a person we trust, and for most of us, that person in the insurance industry is our own agent, the person we call for help with our insurance needs. That relationship must be developed and supported in order to create the needed partnership of insurers and customers.

There are three keys to success in repairing auto insurance: information, individual action, and collective pressure. For each item on the long list of recommendations for how to lower the cost of auto accidents and claims, one or more of these three will be found. Customers must know how their premium dollar is being used and how the imbalances can be corrected. Individuals must be given the power to choose how they will act—in their own risk decisions and on behalf of the community of insurance buyers. And consumers must have the opportunity to support collective action to force changes in the system through changed laws and increased law enforcement.

Principles for Reform

Principle One: The needs of the community of insurance buyers must be paramount.

We have dealt at some length with the concept of community as applied to the group of insurance buyers. The concept is important because the economic interests of the customers are currently neglected. The insurance system, as a mechanism for sharing risk among individuals, creates this community of customers. The members of the community, however, have not been able to control the "destiny" of their own pool of funds. Moreover, while each individual buyer still clearly values the insurance product and the freedom and security it provides, the system as a whole costs more than most buyers want to pay. The total pool of money is not being spent according to the priorities set by the insurance buyers—to help injured people and restore damaged property.

Every party in the insurance process has "rights." Insurance companies, for example, have a constitutional right to make a fair profit. Insurance claimants have a right to fair settlements and fair treatment. Here, though, rights can collide. Claimants have the *right* to go to court, regardless of the size of the loss or nature of the dispute, to gain their settlement. Lawyers have the *right* to file any suit, for any situation, with little or no risk. Doctors and the medical system have the *right* to charge for their services and the *right* to be paid whatever they charge. Auto repair shops have the *right* to price their services and replacement parts and get paid for their work.

Insurance buyers, however, seem to have only the *right* to pay the tab—so far. Everyone involved must come to realize that insurance buyers have a *right* to a say in what they want the premium dollar to pay for, what they want the whole mechanism to accomplish, and what the priorities should be. And they have the *right* to decide who and what will not be paid from the pool of insurance funds. These rights, and the responsibilities that go with them, must be recognized and embraced by the insurance buyers themselves, as well as by politicians, regulators, consumer advocates, and insurance companies.

Respect for the needs of the community of insurance buyers means first that all involved acknowledge that the community exists; second, that it has distinct economic self-interests; and, third, that it has a right to act to protect its economic self-interest.

Principle Two: Individual insurance buyers have the responsibility to act in their own self-interest.

Consumers who are dissatisfied with the way things are can change things. First, they must become informed because it is not enough to complain about lack of legislative action, to be angry and frustrated, and to blame insurance companies for the muddle. Individuals must take responsibility for their own attitudes about insurance, starting by understanding that they need not be helpless victims of the system. They can make a commitment to being part of the solution, to participating in efforts, small or large, that may improve the situation. In this country, every person counts; every vote counts. Although we have become cynical about that old truism, it still holds: an active and vocal member of a community can make a big impact.

As individuals we have it in our power to prevent losses. We can stop a friend from driving drunk; we can drive defensively and safely; we can be demanding consumers by letting our insurance company know we expect a lot, especially information; and we can expect our friends and families to be honest insurance buyers and fair claimants.

As individuals we have it in our power to cut the cost of claims. We can always wear seatbelts; we can be intolerant of inflated claims and fraud and of those who perpetrate them; we can support community and law-enforcement efforts to stop drunk driving, catch auto thieves, and reduce insurance crime; we can let those who would hurt the interests of insurance buyers know our outrage; and we can support legislative proposals that protect our interests as insurance consumers. As insurance buyers, we can demand value for our premium dollars. We have the right to set the priorities for how our funds are spent. When we insist that our voices be heard, change will occur.

Principle Three: The community of insurance buyers, in partnership with insurance companies, has the power to change the system.

We have already stated that change must come in two forms—individual and systemic. The second principle dealt with individual and behavioral change. The third principle suggests how to bring about the systemic changes that must be made to deliver better value to insurance buyers.

Cooperative effort is crucial to social change. We have used the concept of community as a way to describe the cooperative effort necessary among insurance buyers to effect change. We have used the term partnership to describe the relationship between insurers and customers that is necessary to bring about changes to the system.

The excessive legal overhead will never be eliminated from the auto accident claims dollar if we simply blame lawyers for the problem. In fact, lawyer bashing has been singularly unproductive in the fight for legal reform. What will be effective is the conscious choice by insurers and their customers to cut legal overhead by demanding that laws be changed. The present liability system is neither cost efficient nor effective as a means of handling auto accidents claims and treating all claimants fairly. The trial lawyer lobby, however powerful, is only one element in the political equation. A community of insurance buyers no longer willing to pay the legal bill, working with their insurers, could turn the political tide. Legal reform requires that laws be passed, and that requires political action. Political action is the only way of achieving success in cutting legal overhead in auto accident claims—and it is a fight that can be won.

Action by state legislatures is critical to dealing with several other important cost problems. The United States has the most liberal civil justice system of any country in the world in its treatment of noneconomic damages, with the most money paid per capita for pain and suffering and emotional damage. This generous system may be useful to lawyers and some claimants, but is very expensive and wasteful for insurance buyers of all types—especially for auto insurance buyers. Legislative action alone will control these awards, and only widespread political pressure for reform will get the legislatures to act.

Once the economic incentives to build up claims are removed, then insurers and their customers will see far less inflation of claims. The system of paying lawyers on a percentage basis according to the size of the award drives increases in both the amount of economic damages and the amount of noneconomic damages. The United States, one of very few countries to allow fees for lawyers based on a percentage of the award, is also one of the few countries where the vast majority of personal injury cases can be tried before a jury. To change the way lawyers are paid and to keep cases out of court, lawmakers must take action. There is no other way to get at the problems. Again, the means to force that action is through public pressure.

The same is true for enactment and enforcement of drunk-driving laws, increased penalties for claims crime and auto theft, and outlawing duplicate payments. It requires action by lawmakers: public support for such changes is the key.

Citizens have the ability to take control of the political agenda and force change. Californians passed Proposition 103 in the hope that it would change insurance rates. Unfortunately, it dealt with symptoms, not the illnesses of the auto insurance system. Insurance consumers must demand real changes, not ones that only treat the symptoms.

Principle Four: The partnership of customers and insurers will be strengthened by information.

The relationship between trust and information cannot be stressed too much. Consumers need solid information. Consumers cannot make wise choices without adequate information and knowledge about the options. Consumers cannot choose to buy a less damageable car or one less theft-prone without information about the relative cost to repair that car or how often it is stolen. The uninformed consumer is less able to manage his own risks and his own insurance costs.

Insurance industry critics have told consumers for a long time that insurance company greed and inefficiency have caused high auto insurance rates. The fact is that the causes are high claims— too many lawsuits, rising awards for noneconomic damages, fraud, abuse of the claims process, artificially high claims for damages, auto theft, drunk drivers, and the ever-higher cost of repairing cars. Insurance buyers have been deluged with mis-information by those people who take money out of premium payers' pockets but who do not contribute to paying for those claims. Shifting the blame makes sense, of course. The last thing someone who profits from the auto claims system wants is for insurance buyers to take a cold, hard look at where their money is going. Those same insurance buyers just might decide to change things.

Despite the obstacles, repairing the auto insurance system is not hopeless. People with an interest in lower rates for auto insur-ance can get lower rates if they learn and act.

Insurance buyers are members of a community with a unique interest in solving the problem of high costs of auto accident claims. Insurance companies share that interest. A partnership of those two groups is the most effective means of achieving the fundamental goal of customers—to get costs under control.

Bringing about specific solutions to the underlying cost prob-lems will not be simple, of course. The long list of changes that need to be made occupy two entire chapters of this book. The principle for making those proposals work is simple, however: insurance buyers must take matters into their own hands and demand information and a voice in where their premium dollars go. The individual and collective actions of insurance buyers can create the political force to change the auto insurance system.

Trust between insurance consumers and insurance companies will be rebuilt when companies open the flow of information that allows consumers to make better-informed choices about how they deal with risk and at what price. Trust will be reestablished when companies offer consumers a solid relationship with an insurance agent or service representative, the link between the large insurance company and the customer. Trust will be rebuilt when customers see that the partnership between themselves and insurance companies achieves control over the spending of insurance funds, when they see their insurance company as a cost-containment champion. Trust will be rebuilt when consumers are confident that *their* priorities—helping injured people and replacing damaged property—are being met efficiently.

The purpose of insurance has been compromised. Originally, the system was set up to allow people to share the risk of economic misfortune and spread the cost over all members of the insurance-buying community. It was intended to be a tool of self-governance for the individual seeking to deal with risk, to enable the individual to exercise mobility and autonomy, both economic and physical. The present auto insurance system, however, rewards cost-increasing behavior. The solution lies in removing those high-cost incentives and in allowing the principal stake holders, insurers and their customers, to retake control of where the money goes.

NINE

The Agenda

This book has shown the complexity of the auto insurance crisis, exposing where the money goes, the failure of political solutions, the perverse incentives that drive up the cost of claims, and the need to shift from a system of blame to one of responsibility. Most attempts to reform the system have only made things worse. But the system can be changed through the principles set forth in Chapter 8 and the following five-part agenda for auto insurance reform.

Guaranteed Benefits Auto Insurance

The auto insurance system would be much more fair and provide benefits to more people more quickly if every state enacted a law that transformed auto insurance into a guaranteed benefits system. This insurance is a no-fault type that provides every driver with medical benefits and payments for lost wages guaranteed from his own insurance company, regardless of the circumstances of the accident. It would place limits on the ability to sue through a strong verbal threshold, prohibiting use of the legal system unless an injured person suffered permanent and serious injuries or death. The perverse incentives that drive up costs for economic losses, noneconomic damages, and legal expenses would be largely eliminated from the auto insurance dollar.

Low-Income Insurance Voucher System

Low-income drivers would be better able to afford auto insurance if state legislators adopted a program to make insurance vouchers available to drivers who meet an income test. Low-income drivers would be able to drive insured, legally, and at lower cost through purchase of publicly subsidized guaranteed-benefits auto insurance. They would have the freedom to purchase insurance from any company they choose, selecting the benefits and options that fit their needs. They would share responsibility for the cost of insurance and would have an incentive to maintain a safe driving record. The additional cost caused by a low-income driver's poor driving record would not be subsidized. A voucher subsidy system would establish a fair method of assisting low-income drivers in becoming insured, without the incorrect subsidies now found in state programs that admit many drivers who would not qualify under an income test. It would solve the social and political problem associated with many uninsured drivers who cannot afford insurance. A voucher system would also assist all other insured drivers by eliminating subsidies for all drivers who do not merit such public assistance and by decreasing the number of uninsured drivers on the road.

Four Key Systemic Changes:
Drunk Driving, Theft, Fraud, and Auto Repair

Chapter 6 outlined many changes that could be made to lower the cost of auto accident claims. Four basic areas, however, merit special attention:

Drunk driving

Any reduction in alcohol- or drug-impaired driving on our roads will reduce dramatically the number of lives lost, people injured, and property damaged. Any reduction in the toll taken by impaired drivers will also lower the cost of auto insurance. The answer lies in a combination of measures to deter impaired driving, enactment of stricter laws, enforcement of the law, and punishment of offenders, especially repeat offenders. And the public education campaign must be reinvigorated.

Theft

Auto-related theft costs $8 billion a year. Most of that loss is caused by auto-theft criminals. To cut these losses, we must have strict laws and penalties, stepped up enforcement, community involvement, special national programs, and antitheft protection on cars.

Fraud

Insurance fraud comes in as many varieties as ice cream. It ranges from inflating a claim to cover a deductible to conspiring to stage accidents, from creating phony losses to filing frivolous suits. Stemming the tide of insurance claims crime will require a lot of the same tools as cutting theft losses—strict laws and penalties, enforcement, public awareness programs, community involvement, and cooperation of insurance companies with law-enforcement authorities.

Auto repair

The repair and replacement of damaged automobiles consume half of all dollars spent on auto accident claims. What is needed are laws that promote competition among auto parts makers, auto repair shops, and others. We also need more programs that promote quality repairs at reasonable prices and alternative re-pair systems.

Taking Responsibility

To be self-governing means having the responsibility for and the ability to make decisions about how we live our lives—what we learn, how we earn a living, how we spend our money, and what we do with our spare time. Businesses determine what products and services they will provide and price them to compete and to earn a profit. The role of government is to create and oversee rules that ensure fair interchange among individuals, businesses, and other institutions in our democracy. When a dynamic system like auto insurance is not working well and the participants are dissatisfied with the way it is operating or how much it costs, each person who participates in the system has a responsibility to work for change. In the case of auto insurance, insurance companies and insurance agents must lead the reform challenge. They must be joined by each insurance buyer, who should be willing to take individual action. And legislators must respond by enacting laws that uncompromisingly meet the needs of the majority of their constituents.

Rebuilding Trust

Insurance policies are contracts that are supposed to be built on trust—between the insurance buyer and the insurance company. The contract assumes that the buyer will pay the premium and that the company will pay in the event of a loss. But we know that insurance means a lot more than that simple exchange for most Americans. We buy insurance for freedom from fear of financial ruin and for the security of our families and property. Although trust must underlie that insurance contract, we trust people, not institutions. It is critical that the trust underlying the insurance contract be reconnected as a link between human beings—in the relationship between agent and client, in the contact between claimant and company adjuster, in the communication between company and customer, in the consumer information that enables choice, and in the development of community-based approaches to insurance problems.

Notes

1. These independent organizations are the A. M. Best Company, the Insurance Services Office, the National Association of Independent Insurers, and the Insurance Research Council (formerly the All-Industry Research Advisory Council). A. M. Best Company has been in existence for ninety years and publishes a variety of statistical and analytical materials for both the property/casualty and life/health insurance industries. It is widely known as the publisher of the annual *Best's Key Rating Guides,* which rate the financial position of virtually every insurance company doing business in the United States. A. M. Best uses data from each insurance company's sworn annual financial statement as prescribed by the National Association of Insurance Commissioners. Each company must file this statement (NAIC statement) each year with the insurance commissioners in the states in which it does business. The NAIC statement is a comprehensive document that allows state insurance regulators to examine the financial and operating performance of insurers. A. M. Best uses data from the NAIC statement to generate its analysis and rating of companies' financial standings. Supported through subscriptions, Best's publications are used by a wide range of companies and individuals concerned with the financial condition of insurance companies. These publications provide the most complete, accurate, and up-to-date financial and operating information available on the insurance industry.

   The Insurance Services Office (ISO) provides a wide range of rating, actuarial, statistical, and other services relating to property and casualty insurance. ISO offers services to insurance companies and other organizations such as research, policy form development, historical loss data, and related statistical services. ISO works with the National Association of Independent Insurers to produce the ISO/NAII Fast Track Data reports. NAII is a trade association of property, casualty, and surety insurance companies. Both ISO and NAII are supported through fees paid by insurance companies and member subscribers who buy their data services.

The Insurance Research Council (IRC) was formed in 1977 by the property/casualty insurance industry to provide the public and the industry with timely, reliable research information relevant to public policy issues affecting risk and insurance. Until 1990, it was called All-Industry Research Advisory Council (AIRAC). IRC is purely a research organization, publishing findings on a wide range of topics—public attitudes, property losses, auto insurance issues, claims practices, and other subjects. IRC does not serve as a voice for the industry and does not act as an advocate for particular points of view on policy matters. IRC receives its funding from a broad spectrum of trade associations, rating organizations, and individual insurance companies and from sales of its publications.

In contrast to A. M. Best and ISO, whose data is derived from insurance company financial statements and audited filings, many IRC studies, including information about claims payments, are derived from examinations of closed claim files. Closed claim studies are particularly important in the effort to understand where the insurance premium dollar goes. A closed claim study involves the review and documentation of thousands of files of claims that have been settled, providing the most detailed and accurate possible statistics regarding how claim dollars were used, who was paid, and for what injuries or services.

IRC's first study was reported in 1979 in a two-volume work, "Automobile Injuries and Their Compensation in the United States." This study was updated in 1989 based on data from over 46,000 claims closed during 1987. This closed claim study deals only with the amounts paid per claim and provides a very complete and accurate picture of how claims dollars are spent.

2. The consumer coalition included the Consumer Federation of America, Consumers Union, National Insurance Consumer Organization, and Public Citizen. The consumer coalition report's breakdown of 1988 auto insurance dollars, adjusted to the $100 premium format used in Chapter 2, is provided in detail as follows:

Payments for injuries to people

Medical expenses	$9
Lost wages and other economic payments	4
Noneconomic damages, including pain and suffering awards	10
Lawyers' fees (plaintiff only)	7
Subtotal	**30**

Payments for damage to property and cars

Property damage liability	12
Collision claims	18
Comprehensive claims	5
Subtotal	**35**
Total claims payments	**65**

Insurer Expenses

Commissions, and other selling expenses	14
General expense	4
Taxes, licenses, fees	4
Costs of settling claims (including defense lawyers)	9
Total insurer expense	**31**
Claims and expense total	**96**
Premium payment and investment income	**$100**
Net profit after taxes (includes dividends to policyholders)	**$4**

Industry critics have charged auto insurance companies with inefficiency, claiming that they waste too much on overhead, sales commissions, and other administrative expenses. Critics often show statistics indicating that the industry pays only two-thirds of total revenue back to consumers in the form of claims payments.

For comparison, here is the III breakdown of 1988 auto insurance dollars:

Payments for injuries to people

Medical expenses	$10
Lost wages and other economic payments	4
Noneconomic damages, including pain and suffering awards	11
Lawyers' fees (both plaintiff and defense)	10
Other costs of settling injury claims	3
Subtotal	**38**

Payments for damage to property and cars

Property damage liability	13
Collision and comprehensive claims	22
Costs of settling property claims	3
Subtotal	**38**
Total claims and claims expense	**76**

Insurer expenses

Commissions and other selling expenses	14
General expense	4
Taxes, licenses, fees	3
Dividends to policyholders	1
Total insurer expense	**22**
Claims and expense total	**98**
Premium payment and investment income	**$100**
Net profit after taxes	**$2**

For 1988, the III analysis showed $76 spent on claims, whereas the consumer coalition shows only $65 spent on claims. To establish the basis for the difference between these numbers requires a close look at what has been included in the "claims" line and the "expense" line. The most striking difference is where the cost for settling claims is placed. The consumer coalition's figures show the cost of settling claims, including the cost for defense lawyers, as part of insurer overhead. In the III breakdown, the cost of settling claims is included with claims payments and not part of the insurer's operating or selling expense. If the $9 cost of settling claims in the consumer coalition's breakdown is included with claims payments, then these studies differ by only $2 for the total cost of claims and claims expense.

Because the consumer coalition has included the cost of settling claims and legal defense in the insurance companies' overhead, overhead appears as a larger portion of expenditures. This arrangement hides the cost of the legal system and lawyers' fees rather than showing the total effect of the lawsuit system on the cost of claims. These costs are significant, as Chapters 3 and 5 show. Whether the cost of settling claims and defending against suits should be counted as part of claims expense or as part of insurance company overhead is open to debate, but no one could deny that it takes money to handle and settle claims.

The California Department of Insurance study, "Automobile Claims: A Study of Closed Claim Payment Patterns in California," is a review of approximately 40,000 claims closed in 1989 by the state's top eleven insurers. Its breakdown of auto insurance dollars for 1989 is:

Claims and claims expense for personal injury and property	$79
Insurance company expenses, including taxes	22
Total claims and expenses	**101**
Premium payment and investment income	**$100**
Net profit (loss)	**($1)**

Claims and claims-related expenses consumed $79 out of every $100 of insurance revenue in California, compared with $77 in the III national analysis for 1989. Companies showed a net profit nationally of $1, while they lost $1 on California business, in large part because of surging claims costs. The important thing to note is that the California and national studies showed claims and claims expense accounting for nearly the same percentage of total auto insurance dollars.

3. Since early in the twentieth century, the business of insurance has
   been regulated because it has a very important role in the public
   interest. The right of government to regulate the business in that
   public interest was established by the U.S. Supreme Court in
   1914. State regulation of insurance rating practices has been developed and refined ever since. Insurance rate regulation varies
   widely among the states—from a hands-off policy that allows the
   competitive marketplace to establish rates to systems where the
   state actually sets the rates. There is a complete range of regulation systems between these two ends of the spectrum—prior approval laws that require advance approval of a rate before it can
   be used; "file and use" laws that allow insurers to use rates upon
   filing but make them subject to review by the regulator; "flex"
   rating laws that allow insurers to change rates within a specified
   percentage range without seeking prior approval; and "use and
   file" systems that allow an insurer to use a rate and file it with the
   regulator for information purposes.

4. The traditional liability system is based on the concept of fault. Someone who is injured in an auto accident will sue the other driver
   because the accident was "his fault." If someone runs a stop sign
   and crashes into someone else's car, he is "at fault" in the accident and will be held responsible for the cost of injuries to the
   passengers of the other car and for repair costs to the other auto.
   His liability insurance will pay for those costs. And if the other
   driver sues, the liability insurance of the one "at fault" will pay
   the cost of his legal defense.

   In cases where fault is very clear and one party admits his
   responsibility, there is very little need for use of the legal system.
   The party who admits fault and takes responsibility for the damage will endeavor to fulfill his responsibility directly and quickly.

   But what about all those accidents where it is not clear who
   was at fault? What about the accident when one driver misses a
   stop sign but the other driver was speeding and may have contributed to the two drivers' inability to avoid a collision? What
   about the situation where no one admits responsibility for the
   accident? That is when the legal system gets involved. The civil
   justice system is then charged with the task of determining how
   "justice" will be established. The court will have to decide who
   was principally at fault. The lawyers on each side of the argu-

ment will seek to have someone else held responsible for paying the damages. That is their job.

This is the key purpose of the lawsuit system when auto accident cases are the issue. The court is the means used to decide who is responsible and then how much the responsible party must pay to others. Liability for losses is determined based on a judgment regarding who was at fault. Our liability system is a fault-based system. The system is designed to resolve the dispute about who has to pay. Presumably, the one not at fault does not have to pay.

Bibliography

Agnew, J. Scott, and Don Marshall. *Current Award Trends in Personal Injury*. Solon, Ohio: Jury Verdict Research, Inc., 1990.

All-Industry Research Advisory Council. *Automobile Injuries and Their Compensation in the United States*. Vol. 1 and 2. Oak Brook, Ill.: All-Industry Research Advisory Council, 1979.

———. *Claimant Satisfaction in Auto Accident Cases*. Oak Brook, Ill.: All-Industry Research Advisory Council, 1989.

———. *Compensation for Automobile Injuries in the United States*. Oak Brook, Ill.: All-Industry Research Advisory Council, 1989.

———. *The Cost of Auto Insurance: How Consumer Choices and Characteristics Affect the Premiums People Pay*. Oak Brook, Ill.: All-Industry Research Advisory Council, 1980.

———. *Crime Losses in Property Casualty Insurance*. Oak Brook, Ill.: All-Industry Research Advisory Council, 1984.

———. *Patterns of Shopping Behavior in Auto Insurance*. Oak Brook, Ill.: All-Industry Research Advisory Council, 1985.

———. *Public Attitude Monitor*. Oak Brook, Ill.: All-Industry Research Advisory Council, 1986, 1987, 1988, 1989.

———. *Special Investigative Units: Surveys on Insurance Company Use of SIUs for Fraud Investigations*. Oak Brook, Ill.: All-Industry Research Advisory Council, 1984.

———. *State Motor Vehicle Records as a Source of Driver Performance Information*. Oak Brook, Ill.: All-Industry Research Advisory Council, 1981.

———. *Uninsured Motorists*. Oak Brook, Ill.: All-Industry Research Advisory Council, 1989.

———. *Uninsured Motorist Facts and Figures*. Oak Brook, Ill.: All-Industry Research Advisory Council, 1984.

Allen, Michael. "More Car Owners Are Scheming to Cheat Insurance Companies as Economy Falters." *Wall Street Journal*, October 10, 1990.

Alliance of American Insurers. *Auto Insurance: A Public Policy for the 1990s.* Schaumburg, Ill.: Alliance of American Insurers, 1989.

———. *Auto Theft Facts and Figures—1988.* Schaumburg, Ill.: Alliance of American Insurers, 1989.

———. *Special Issue: Competitive Replacement Parts.* Schaumburg, Ill.: Alliance of American Insurers, 1990.

American Automobile Association. *Auto Insurance: What Is the Crisis? What Can Consumers Do?* Heathrow, Fla.: American Automobile Association, 1990.

American Insurance Association. *Auto Reform Plan.* Washington, D.C.: American Insurance Association, 1989.

Baldwin, Ben G. *The Complete Book of Insurance: Protecting Your Life, Health, Property & Income.* Chicago, Ill.: Probus Publishing Company, 1989.

Beauchemin, Timothy A., and Orin S. Kramer. "Auto Insurance: The Right Road to Reform." *The State Factor* 15, no. 2, Washington, D.C.: American Legislative Exchange Council, 1989.

A.M. Best Company. "Average Auto Premiums by State—1988." *Best's Insurance Management Reports,* Financial News, On-Line Reports, Property/Casualty Release no. 4. Oldwick, N.J.: A.M. Best Company, 1990.

———. *Best's Key Rating Guide: Property-Casualty 1990.* Oldwick, N.J.: A. M. Best Company, 1990.

———. "Private Passenger Auto Profitability." *Best's Insurance Management Reports,* Financial News, On-Line Reports, Property/Casualty Release no. 4. Oldwick, N.J.: A.M. Best Company, 1989.

Brobeck, Stephen. "U.S. Consumer Knowledge: The Results of a Nationwide Test." Report from a Test Conducted by the Educational Testing Service, Washington, D.C., Consumer Federation of America, 1990.

California Citizens Commission on Tort Reform. *Righting the Liability Balance.* California Citizens Commission on Tort Reform, 1977.

California Department of Insurance. *Automobile Claims: A Study of Closed Claim Payment Patterns in California.* San Francisco, Calif.: California Department of Insurance, 1990.

―――. *California Private Passenger Auto Insurance Premium Survey.* San Francisco, Calif.: California Department of Insurance, 1988.

―――. *Preliminary Report—Private Passenger Automobile Liability Experience by Zip Code.* San Francisco, Calif.: California Department of Insurance, 1988.

California Trial Lawyers Association. *No-Fault: Adding Insult to Injury.* Sacramento, Calif.: California Trial Lawyers Association, 1989.

Consumer Federation of America, Consumers Union, National Insurance Consumer Organization, and Public Citizen. *Reducing Auto Insurance Rates: A Comprehensive Program.* Washington, D.C.: Consumer Federation of America, 1989.

Consumer Reports Magazine. "Auto Insurance: What Coverages Do You Need? Which Companies Offer Better Service? Which Companies Offer Lower Premiums?" October 1988.

El-Gasseir, Mohamed M. *The Potential Benefits and Workability of Pay-As-You-Drive Automobile Insurance.* El Monte, Calif.: State of California Energy Resources Conservation and Development Commission, 1990.

Flick, Rachel. "Why Lawyers Hate No-Fault." *Reader's Digest,* June 1990.

Frahm, Donald R. "Ten Causes of High Auto Premiums—and Their Cures." *Hartford Agent* 81, no. 6, 1990.

Green, Thomas E., editor. *Glossary of Insurance Terms.* 3d ed. Santa Monica, Calif.: Merritt Company, 1987.

Hammit, James K. *Automobile Accident Compensation.* Vol. 2, *Payments by Auto Insurers.* Santa Monica, Calif.: Institute for Civil Justice, Rand Corporation, 1985.

Hammit, James K., Robert L. Houchens, Sandra S. Polin, and John Rolph. *Automobile Accident Compensation.* Vol. 4, *State Rules.* Santa Monica, Calif.: Institute for Civil Justice, Rand Corporation, 1985.

Hammit, James K., and John E. Rolph. *Limiting Liability for Automobile Accidents: Are No-Fault Tort Thresholds Effective?* Santa Monica, Calif.: Institute for Civil Justice, Rand Corporation, 1985.

Hampden-Turner, Charles M. "The Quest for the Great White Whale or How Attempts to Tame a Living System Can Get You Deeper and Deeper into Trouble." A Report on the New Jersey Automobile Full Insurance Underwriting Association. Worcester, Mass.: Hanover Insurance Company, 1990.

Harrington, Scott E. "Competition and Regulation in the Automobile Insurance Industry Market." University of South Carolina, June 1990.

Hasse, Paul. *Auto Insurance Reform in America: A New Dynamic.* San Francisco, Calif.: McKinsey & Company, Inc., 1990.

Heiden, Edward J., and Thomas M Lenard. *Consumer Savings from No-Fault Automobile Insurance.* Washington, D.C.: Heiden Associates, for Project New Start, 1989.

Hensler, D., M. Vaiana, J. Kakalik, and M. Peterson. *Trends in Tort Litigation: The Story behind the Statistics.* Santa Monica, Calif.: Institute for Civil Justice, Rand Corporation, 1987.

Highway Loss Data Institute. "Injury and Collision Loss Experience." Washington, D.C.: Highway Loss Data Institute, 1988.

Highway Users Federation and Automotive Safety Foundation. *Programs to Reduce Alcohol and Other Drug Impaired Driving.* Washington, D.C.: Highway Users Federation for Safety, 1988.

Hingson, Ralph W., Jonathan Howland, and Suzette Levenson. "Effects of Legislative Reform to Reduce Drunken Driving and Alcohol-related Traffic Fatalities." *Public Health Reports* 103, no. 6, Nov.–Dec. 1988.

Houchens, Robert L. *Automobile Accident Compensation.* Vol. 3, *Payments from All Sources.* Santa Monica, Calif.: Institute for Civil Justice, Rand Corporation, 1985.

Huber, Peter W. *Liability: The Legal Revolution and Its Consequences.* New York, N.Y.: Basic Books, Inc., 1988.

Insurance Industry Initiative Campaign Committee Research Committee. *Auto Injury Claims: California Compared to Other Selected States.*

Sacramento, Calif.: Insurance Industry Initiative Campaign Committee, April 1988.

Insurance Information Institute. *Air Bags: A Matter of Life or Death.* New York, N.Y.: Insurance Information Institute, 1984.

―――. *Auto Insurance Issues.* New York, N.Y.: Insurance Information Institute, 1989.

―――. "Auto Safety and Crashworthiness." *Data Base Reports.* New York, N.Y.: Insurance Information Institute, 1989.

―――. "Auto Theft and Insurance Fraud." *Data Base Reports.* New York, N.Y.: Insurance Information Institute, 1988.

―――. "Compulsory Auto Insurance." *Data Base Reports.* New York, N.Y.: Insurance Information Institute, 1989.

―――. "Drunk Driving." *Data Base Reports.* New York, N.Y.: Insurance Information Institute, 1989.

―――. *Drunk Driving: A Killer We Can Stop.* New York, N.Y.: Insurance Information Institute, 1989.

―――. *The Fact Book: 1990 Property/Casualty Insurance Facts.* New York, N.Y.: Insurance Information Institute, 1990.

―――. "No-Fault Auto Insurance." *Data Base Reports.* New York, N.Y.: Insurance Information Institute, 1989.

―――. "Rate Regulation." *Data Base Reports.* New York, N.Y.: Insurance Information Institute, 1989.

―――. "Residual Markets." *Data Base Reports.* New York, N.Y.: Insurance Information Institute, 1988.

―――. *Sharing the Risk: How the Nation's Businesses, Homes and Autos Are Insured.* 3d ed. New York, N.Y.: Insurance Information Institute, 1989.

―――. *Two Minutes on Insurance: Why the Cost of Personal Auto Insurance Is Rising; Tort Reform and Insurance Prices; Solutions to the Lawsuit Crisis; Is There Really a Lawsuit Crisis?* New York, N.Y.: Insurance Information Institute, 1987, 1988.

―――. "Where the Auto Insurance Premium Dollar Goes, 1988." *Executive Letter Special Report.* New York, N.Y.: Insurance Information Institute, 1989.

————. "Where the Auto Insurance Premium Dollar Goes, 1989." *Executive Letter Special Report*. New York, N.Y.: Insurance Information Institute, 1990.

Insurance Institute for Highway Safety. "Alcohol," "Elderly," "Motorcycles," "Occupants," "Pedestrians," "Roadside Hazards," "Teenagers," and "Vehicle Size." *IIHS Facts 1988*. Washington, D.C.: Insurance Institute for Highway Safety, 1988.

————. *Auto Insurance Losses Driven by Repair Costs, Car Size, Urbanization*. Arlington, Va.: Insurance Institute for Highway Safety, 1988.

————. *A Practical Agenda for Highway Safety: State and Federal Actions*. Arlington, Va.: Insurance Institute for Highway Safety, 1989.

Insurance Marketing Services. "Government-Run Auto Insurance Programs: One That Works!" Transcript of teleconference, Santa Monica, Calif.: June 1990.

Insurance Research Council (formerly, All-Industry Research Advisory Council). *Attorney Involvement in Auto Injury Claims*. Oak Brook, Ill.: All-Industry Research Advisory Council, 1988.

————. *Auto Insurance Reform*. Oak Brook, Ill.: Insurance Research Council, 1990.

————. *Trends in Auto Bodily Injury Claims*. Oak Brook, Ill.: Insurance Research Council, 1990.

Insurance Services Office, Inc. *Factors Affecting Urban Auto Insurance Costs*. New York, N.Y.: Insurance Services Office, Inc., 1988.

————. *Personal Auto Insurance: Costs and Profits in Perspective*. New York, N.Y.: Insurance Services Office, Inc., 1989.

Ippolito, Richard A. "The Effects of Price Regulation in the Automobile Insurance Industry." *Journal of Law and Economics* 22, no. 1, April 1979.

Kittel, John. "Auto Insurance: Defusing the Bomb." *Best's Review,* May 1990.

Kramer, Orin. *Introduction to the Auto Insurance Affordability Problem*. Presentation to the National Conference on Auto Insurance Issues, Alexandria, Va.: Insurance Information Institute, 1989.

———. *Where Every Insurance Dollar Goes.* Presentation to the National Conference on Auto Insurance Issues, Alexandria, Va.: Insurance Information Institute, 1989.

Mooney, Sean. *Auto Insurance: Critical Choices for the 1990s.* New York, N.Y.: Insurance Information Institute, 1989.

Nader, Ralph, and Wesley J. Smith. *Winning the Insurance Game: The Complete Consumer's Guide to Saving Money.* New York, N.Y.: Knightsbridge Publishing Company, 1990.

National Association of Independent Insurers. *Containing Auto Insurance Costs: A Public Policy Plan.* Des Plaines, Ill.: National Association of Independent Insurers, 1990.

National Association of Professional Insurance Agents/Consumer Insurance Interest Group. *Factors Contributing to Auto Insurance Claims Costs: A White Paper Summary of Recommendations.* Alexandria, Va.: National Association of Professional Insurance Agents, 1989.

National Automobile Theft Bureau. *Annual Report 1989.* Palos Hills, Ill.: National Automobile Theft Bureau, 1990.

National Highway Traffic Safety Administration. *Compensating Auto Accident Victims: A Follow-up Report on No-Fault Auto Insurance Experiences.* Washington, D.C.: U.S. Department of Transportation, 1985.

———. *The Economic Cost to Society of Motor Vehicle Accidents.* Washington, D.C.: U.S. Department of Transportation, 1983.

———. *The Economic Cost to Society of Motor Vehicle Accidents, Addendum.* Washington, D.C.: U.S. Department of Transportation, 1987.

National Insurance Consumer Organization. *How to Cut Auto Insurance Rates by 25 percent: A Four-Part Plan.* Alexandria, Va.: National Insurance Consumer Organization, 1988.

O'Connell, Jeffrey. "Alternatives to the Tort System for Personal Injury." University of Virginia, January 1986.

O'Connell, Jeffrey, and Robert H. Joost. "Giving Motorists a Choice between Fault and No-Fault Insurance." *Virginia Law Review* 72, 1986.

Public Citizen. *Auto Insurance Fact Sheet.* Washington, D.C.: Public Citizen, 1989.

————. *The Problem with No-Fault Auto Insurance*. Washington, D.C.: Public Citizen, 1990.

Rolph, John E., James K. Hammit, Robert L. Houchens, and Sandra Polin. *Automobile Accident Compensation*. Vol. 1, *Who Pays How Much How Soon?* Santa Monica, Calif.: Institute for Civil Justice, Rand Corporation, 1985.

Spiro, Peter, and Daniel Mirvish. "Whose No-Fault Is It, Anyway?" *Washington Monthly*, October 1989.

Taylor, Barbara J. *How to Get Your Money's Worth in Home and Auto Insurance*. New York, N.Y.: McGraw-Hill, Inc., 1990.

U.S. Congress. House. Statement of Ralph Nader on Proposition 103 before the House Subcommittee on Commerce, Consumer Protection and Competitiveness. December 6, 1988.

U.S. Department of Transportation. *Compensating Auto Accident Victims: A Follow-Up Report on No-Fault Auto Insurance Experiences*. U.S. Department of Transportation, May 1985.

U.S. General Accounting Office. *Auto Insurance: State Regulation Affects Cost and Viability*. U.S. General Accounting Office, 1986.

U.S. Justice Department. *Report of the Tort Policy Working Group on the Causes, Extent and Policy Implications of the Current Crisis in Insurance Availability and Affordability*. U. S. Justice Department, February 1986.

Vaughan, Emmett J., and Terri M. Vaughan. "Proposition 103: Repealing the Law of Supply." *CPCU Journal* 43, no. 1, 1990.

Washington State Department of Insurance. *The Cost of Auto Insurance: A Study Comparing Automobile Insurance Premiums to Factors Which Affect the Price We Pay*. Olympia, Wash.: Washington State Department of Insurance, 1988.

Western Insurance Information Service. *Key Facts on Auto Insurance Costs in California*. New York, N.Y.: Insurance Information Institute, 1988.

————. "Auto Accident Litigation Index." *Insurance Journal*, September 4, 1989.

Zinkewicz, Phil. "The Personal Auto Mess." *Independent Agent*. Alexandria, Va.: Independent Insurance Agents of America, June 1990.

Index